HOW TO GET
FROM WHERE
YOU ARE
TO WHERE YOU
WANT TO BE

Also by Cheri Huber

From *Keep It Simple Books:*

The Key and the Name of the Key Is Willingness

How You Do Anything Is How You Do Everything: A Workbook

*The Depression Book: Depression As an Opportunity
for Spiritual Growth* (rev. ed.)

There Is Nothing Wrong with You: Going Beyond Self-Hate

The Fear Book: Facing Fear Once and for All

Nothing Happens Next: Responses to Questions about Meditation

Be the Person You Want to Find: Relationship and Self-Discovery

Sex and Money . . . are dirty, aren't they?

From *A Center for the Practice of Zen Buddhist Meditation:*

That Which You Are Seeking Is Causing You to Seek

Time-Out for Parents: A Compassionate Approach to Parenting

From *Present Perfect Books* (Sara Jenkins, editor):

Trying to Be Human: Zen Talks from Cheri Huber

*Turning Toward Happiness: Conversations with a
Zen Teacher and Her Students*

Good Life: A Zen Precepts Retreat with Cheri Huber

Buddha Facing the Wall: Interviews with American Zen Monks

Sweet Zen: Dharma Talks with Cheri Huber

※   ※   ※

All of the above are available at your local bookstore,
or may be ordered by visiting:

Hay House USA: **www.hayhouse.com**
Hay House Australia: **www.hayhouse.com.au**
Hay House UK: **www.hayhouse.co.uk**
Hay House South Africa: **orders@psdprom.co.za**

HOW to GET
FROM WHERE
YOU ARE
TO WHERE YOU
WANT to BE

Cheri Huber

HAY HOUSE, INC.
Carlsbad, California
London • Sydney • Johannesburg
Vancouver • Hong Kong

Published and distributed in the United States by: Hay House, Inc., P.O. Box 5100, Carlsbad, CA 92018-5100 • Phone: (760) 431-7695 or (800) 654-5126 • Fax: (760) 431-6948 or (800) 650-5115 • www.hayhouse.com • **Published and distributed in Australia by:** Hay House Australia Pty. Ltd., 18/36 Ralph St., Alexandria NSW 2015 • *Phone:* 612-9669-4299 • *Fax:* 612-9669-4144 • www.hayhouse.com.au • **Published and distributed in the United Kingdom by:** Hay House UK, Ltd. • Unit 62, Canalot Studios • 222 Kensal Rd., London W10 5BN • *Phone:* 44-20-8962-1230 • Fax: 44-20-8962-1239 • www.hayhouse.co.uk • **Published and distributed in the Republic of South Africa by:** Hay House SA (Pty), Ltd., P.O. Box 990, Witkoppen 2068 • Phone/Fax: 2711-7012233 • orders@psdprom.co.za • **Distributed in Canada by:** Raincoast • 9050 Shaughnessy St., Vancouver, B.C. V6P 6E5 • *Phone:* (604) 323-7100 • *Fax:* (604) 323-2600

Editorial: Sara Jenkins, Jill Kramer • *Design:* Jenny Richards
Photo of Cheri Huber: © 2000 Jane Lidz

The author of this book does not dispense medical advice or prescribe the use of any technique as a form of treatment for physical or medical problems without the advice of a physician, either directly or indirectly. The intent of the author is only to offer information of a general nature to help you in your quest for emotional and spiritual well-being. In the event you use any of the information in this book for yourself, which is your constitutional right, the author and the publisher assume no responsibility for your actions.

Library of Congress Cataloging-in-Publication Data

Huber, Cheri.
    How to get from where you are to where you want to be / Cheri Huber.
      p. cm.
    ISBN 1-56170-715-5 (tradepaper)
      1. Spiritual life—Zen Buddhism. 2. Change (Psychology)—Religious aspects—Buddhism. I. Title.

    BQ9286.2 .H83 2000
    294.3'444—dc21   00-037041

ISBN 1-56170-715-5

08 07 06 05   7 6 5 4
1st printing, October 2000
4th printing, January 2005

Printed in the United States of America

❄ ❄ ❄

For Monique and Brian,
my sweetest experience
of unconditional love

❄ ❄ ❄

Contents

*"Why should the mind be burdened with opinions at all,
with what you think about this or that person, or book,
or idea? Why shouldn't the mind be empty?
Only when it is empty can it see clearly."*
— J. Krishnamurti, *The Only Revolution*

❊ PREFACE ❊

Earlier in my life, I read many wonderful, informative books about what is possible for us. I was inspired and enlightened by them. But in each case, the inspiration faded, and I was essentially left in the same place I started—with only a little more intellectual understanding, and a stronger belief that I should somehow be "different" as a result of having that information. But I wasn't different in any significant way. I still wasn't able to be the person I felt I was capable of being. I didn't know *how* to be that person, and none of the books I read helped much.

I knew I wanted something more. I knew I was not happy and wanted to be happy. I knew I was tied in knots and wanted to be free. I knew I was suffering and wanted not to suffer. But I did not know *how*.

My own awareness practice has been devoted to putting into words the *process*, the *how*. For years I did not put my name on the books I wrote because I didn't want people to focus on me as a personality, but rather, to focus on the practice. I did not tell the story of my own search for fear that those reading it would simply use it as one more unhelpful comparison. However, that way of doing things merely separated me from those with whom I actually wanted to connect.

This book is my best effort to lay out in a step-by-step format the process that will take you from where you are to where you want to be. Elements of my story appear throughout the book to illustrate the fact that waking up, letting go of what is keeping one stuck, and stepping free of the misery of the past is available to each of us—regardless of our circumstances. We all struggle, and life is challenging for everyone. Yet each of us has everything we need to overcome whatever obstacles we encounter. Anyone can do it; it just takes willingness and practice.

❋ ACKNOWLEDGMENTS ❋

I wish to thank all those who have honored me by attending the classes, workshops, and retreats I have offered over the last 25 years. This book would not exist without your contributions.

Thank you to all my teachers, titled and untitled.

Thank you to my brilliant editors.

And a very special thank you to Danny.

"Whether one is Catholic, or a Muslim, or Hindu, or a Communist, the propaganda of a hundred, two hundred, or five thousand years is part of [the] verbal structure of images which goes to make up our consciousness. We are conditioned by what we eat, by the economic pressures, by the culture and society in which we live. We are that culture, we are that society. Merely to revolt against it is to revolt against ourselves. If you rebel against yourself, not knowing what you are, your rebellion is utterly wasted. But to be aware, without condemnation, of what you are—such awareness brings about action which is entirely different from the action of a reformer or a revolutionary."

— J. Krishnamurti

CHAPTER ONE

INTRODUCTION: A New Direction

Where I've Come From

In 1944, on my first birthday, my father lay in the hospital with a brain tumor. The doctors knew they had to operate if he was to have any chance at all, but they had no confidence that he would survive the surgery. "We just don't know, Mrs. Philbrook," they told my frantic mother. "This is experimental surgery, and we cannot give you a guarantee about the outcome."

My mother would leave that hospital and take a bus across town to where my brother, age three, lay in another hospital, so thin that his knees and elbows looked like doorknobs held together with lengths of bone, huge red sores all over his emaciated body. "We just don't know, Mrs. Philbrook," the doctors there told her. "We've done all the tests, but we don't know what's wrong."

Then my mother would come back to care for me. I don't know what arrangements she made for my care in her absence; I only know what she told me later—how at that early stage in my life, I seemed to experience the misery of abandonment. Unable to explain the terrible demands on her life at that time, Mother would rock me and sob. She was only 30 years old, facing widowhood and the death of her oldest child—and pregnant with her third baby.

Only a few years before, my maternal grandmother had committed suicide. Her alcoholic husband, my grandfather, had taken a job in Needles, California, one of the hottest places on the planet. My grandmother, her body covered with the eczema that had plagued her all her life, simply couldn't face the prospect of month after month of 100- to115-degree weather. One morning when the family had left for work and school, she put a rifle to her chest and pulled the trigger. Finally, my grandfather stopped drinking.

❈   ❈   ❈

Thirty years later, I woke up in a hospital room two weeks after putting a rifle to my midsection and pulling the trigger. I opened my eyes and finally managed to focus on what turned out to be a man leaning over me. He was the surgeon who had saved my life. Dangling from his lips was a cigarette containing the longest ash I had ever seen. I was fascinated by that ash, watching it move up and down, back and forth, as he talked, wondering when it would fall, wondering if he had dropped one of those ashes inside me as he was sewing me up.

"I don't know how you lived through this," he announced, with a great deal of energy that sounded to me like anger. "That bullet should have killed you. I would suggest that you find out why you're alive." He saved my life in the operating room, but much more significantly, I know that he saved my life with that terse speech.

No one had ever spoken to me in that way. I was familiar with getting information—with strong feelings attached—that I should do or be something because it benefited the person giving the information. But this clearly wasn't to benefit *him*. This was to benefit *me*.

Lying in that hospital bed, I began thinking, through a haze of morphine, about what the surgeon had said. I had spent my whole life trying to do what people wanted me to do, failing miserably. It may not have seemed so to others, but I really had put forward my best effort to fit in.

※　※　※

I was learning disabled, but that was before the term became common, back in the days when intelligent kids not doing well in school were said to have a "bad attitude." I don't think I ever got a report card that didn't say, "Cheryl is not working up to her potential." I can remember sitting at the kitchen table night after night trying to do math problems, unable to get them right, and finally throwing the book across the room in frustration. Then the teacher would send home a note that said, "Cheryl isn't trying." I gave up on teachers, school, education, and experts in general. I gave up on the system, but I never quit trying.

I had received all the right messages about how I should go to school, get good grades, go to a good college, get a good job, meet the right guy, get married, have kids, bring them up, and save money for retirement. But I couldn't believe that people really thought that was all there was to life. *I* had noticed—and therefore could not imagine that others had not noticed—that we human beings have some pretty big problems in front of us— problems that make retirement look like nothing. Here we are rocketing around in space on this clod of dirt. We don't know how we got here, what we're doing here, where we're going, or what's going to happen to us. *Hasn't anyone noticed that?*

I got really nervous when I realized that if people *had* noticed, they didn't seem to express the concern that I thought the situation warranted. *You're going to die!* I don't care how much money you make or save, you're going to die!

I was clearly the odd person out—this was before the

1960s—and it seemed in my best interest to try to get going in the same general direction as the crowd. I went on to college, but lost what little enthusiasm I had for that venture when my mother died. I was 18. I had already met a guy—maybe not the *right* guy, but at least a *right enough* guy, so we got married and started the requisite family.

When I began to suspect that what was wrong with me was manic depression and learned that that disorder runs in families, a good number of things fell into place. I realized that in addition to the difficulties life had handed her, my mother must have been dealing with this debilitating condition. I felt great sympathy for my grandmother's inability to face such a dismal future. I could see that my uncle's alcoholism masked *his* depression. I realized that my aunt's compulsive eating was *her* way of dealing with her depression. We were a depression "stream" going back as far as anyone could remember. When I looked at the various ways in which my family had chosen to handle our "problem," I decided that my grandmother had had the best idea.

❄ ❄ ❄

As I lay in that hospital bed, it occurred to me that although I had put a lot of effort into doing what I was *supposed* to do, what I had never tried to do was be happy. I had worked so very hard to do the things that people implied would lead to happiness, but I had never been happy. I had been angry, guilty, sad, confused, and overwhelmed—but never happy. I decided to see if I could be.

I wanted to know two things: how other people handled this "rocketing around on a clod of dirt" situation, and how people managed to be happy in spite of the uncertainty of life. I thought that the world of philosophy would be a good place to begin.

I read philosophy from the Greeks to the present, and I found a lot of interesting ideas and pertinent questions. But it was clear that ultimately they were in the same boat with me: They did not know how things worked, and they did not seem all that happy with what they supposedly *did* know. I phrase it in that way because it was obvious to me that there was an awful lot of speculation passing for knowledge.

My next stop was the world of religion. Having been raised without any religious background, religion had always fascinated me. In my early teens, I badgered friends to take me along to the churches their parents made them attend. Only one of my friends was sincere about her religion and went to church by choice. I was intrigued by that, and I admired the way she lived from her beliefs. I wished I could be that way but knew I could not make myself believe, no matter how hard I tried. I was deeply disappointed, because I *wanted* to believe.

Soon I left Western religion behind and went looking toward the East. My first stop was India and the aphorisms of Patanjali. Wonderful, but nothing I was moved to pursue. With the Sufis, while I loved the poetry and could sense the wisdom, I didn't feel inclined to go deeper.

Buddhism seemed the strangest of all—although the story of the Buddha did sound a lot like the story of Jesus, just without the "Son of God" aspect. Again, parts of it were attractive, but I couldn't imagine *believing* it.

A little book by D. T. Suzuki introduced me to Zen. I had read references to this practice and had a sense of its mystery, but I had never encountered it directly. When I picked up that book and read the first paragraph, my breath quickened. As I began the second paragraph, I realized that I had stopped breathing; I was holding my breath. My heart was beating fast—I was excited, thrilled, high. I raced on, my hands trembling. Never had I experienced anything like it. It dawned on me that I had no idea what the author was talking about! *But I knew he knew* what he was talking about, and I knew he knew what I wanted to know. Yes! That was what I'd been looking for!

But—now what? How to proceed? Would I need to go to Japan?

As it turned out, in that wonderfully weird way of life at some points, there was a Zen monastery less than 25 miles from where I lived. In the early 1970s, when there were only a handful of Zen monasteries in the country, and only a few books on the subject in English, how could there be a Zen monastery a few miles up the road from the podunk village where I was living? I have always filed that remarkable circumstance under "Blessings abound."

From the moment I walked onto the monastery property and met the Zen master who became my teacher, I never wanted to do anything with my life except practice awareness. The practice of awareness has changed my life, put an end to my suffering—and has brought me the happiness I sought.

❀ ❀ ❀

My passion for Zen, for awareness, has only grown over the years. I owe my life to this practice, and my life is dedicated to assisting anyone who chooses to practice for themselves the process of awakening and putting an end to suffering.

In this book, I have attempted to present the necessary steps in that process, as well as articulate the attitude of mind required for the journey. I will describe significant junctures in my own journey, the points at which these various steps became available to me. I will also share with you stories of others who have followed this path and have managed to extricate themselves from the ignorance and delusion that had kept them in the bondage of suffering.

I invite you to join me on this journey. If you follow the process outlined here, I can promise you this: It will work. My start in life was as inauspicious as that of anyone who will be attempting the journey, and if *I* can reach a place of freedom, *anyone* can. People meet me today and think that life has always been easy for me. They assume that I didn't have to go through the kinds of life problems they face. No matter how often I tell them that I have, indeed, "been there," all they can see is the person I am today. I assure you I have taken each painful, terrifying step along this path to reach the place where I am now, and I have great confidence that if I am graced with more years on this planet, I will have the opportunity to take many more such steps.

Life is a process. If we learn to enjoy the process, life is an enjoyable journey. If we remain in ignorance and delusion, life is filled with suffering. There is nothing to fear in awareness. Awareness only makes life better.

And here is the greatest secret I can offer you: If you go through life with someone who loves you, who sympathizes with you, and who has compassion for your struggles, life will be a joy-filled, exciting adventure. We each have *within us* what it takes to be the wise, compassionate, loving presence we have wished and longed for. The Buddha said, "You must work out your own salvation diligently." We each need to be saved, and we each are that which can save us. This is not something to wish for, to hope for, or even to believe in. This is an actual moment-by-moment experience that is available to all of us. More than that: It is our birthright.

So, with this book, I offer to others the basic elements in the awareness practice that has so profoundly changed my life. I invite you to take an active role in the process of developing a deeper, clearer awareness of how you operate in life—and how to go beyond what prevents you from having and being what you want.

Wanting to Change

If you are like most people, you have decided to read this book because you want to change. There is something different you want to *do* or *have* or *be* or *get*.

We are socially engineered creatures, and trying to be different is what we do. We want to be thinner, fitter, richer, more generous, less anxious; we want to work less, complete projects, learn new skills, feel more excitement, forgive the past, let go of a habit, have more enthusiasm, feel loved, be more loving, be more energetic, be content, be in love, be happy, enjoy life more—fill in whatever it is that you want to change about your life. Attempting to gain control of ourselves, our lives, and even the lives of others is a human obsession. Of course it's not an accident that we're obsessed with change and control. As children, we learned early and often that how we are, as we are, is not okay. We are subjected to social engineering in the form of conditioning, because as we were when we arrived, we were not acceptable to society.

My image for our struggle to see ourselves clearly, to recognize who we are and what we have been taught, to let go of the erroneous and extraneous, and learn to accept ourselves, is "socks in a washer." All those socks are so intertwined, going every which way, that they're impossible to sort out. If you want any clarity on those socks, you need to separate them, pull them away from one another, and lay them out. As soon as you do so, you can see which is which and what goes with what. The same is true for the tangled ball of conditioned beliefs, assumptions, aspects of the personality, and unexamined projections that each of us has learned to call "I."

We tend to be spectators more than participants. Sports, movies, television, and Internet surfing encourage us to sit back, relax, and be entertained. The process of bringing conscious, compassionate awareness to a socially conditioned life, however, definitely requires active audience participation. A strictly intellectual understanding of the process of life is as meaningful as an intellectual understanding of flying or parenting. If you want to take full advantage of the impulse that caused you to pick this book up, I strongly encourage you to do all the work as suggested.

❀　❀　❀

In addition to teaching this process in workshops, meditation retreats, and at our Zen Monastery Practice Center, recently I also offered the opportunity for a large number of people to participate in two daily e-mail workshops, one ten months in duration, the other two months. These workshops were "interactive" in a low-tech sort of way—that is, people would read what was e-mailed to them each day, respond if they wished, and some of those responses would be made available for the other participants. Many of the personal accounts included in this book are from those workshops, along with questions, observations, and stories from other students I have worked with (all names have been changed). I hope their words, as well as mine, will encourage you to question, observe, and respond for yourself as a way of making this practice your own.

Language for the Journey

As with any foray into foreign territory, it can be helpful to learn the language of the natives. In this practice, you will encounter terms and phrasing that differ from customary patterns of expression. We intentionally use language in these ways to make certain points. At first it can sound like jargon, but I ask you to keep this in mind: We are searching for words that will communicate that which is outside our normal way of perceiving. If we use the same old words, we are stuck with the same old meanings, and that leaves us in the same old places. To draw our attention to a new and different perception, we use words that help catapult us out of the habitual world of everyday reality and into the fresh, awake, aliveness of the present moment.

Conditioning: The internal programming by which an individual is turned into a person who will fit into a given culture. The conditioning process is initiated (usually unconsciously) by a child's primary caregivers, and continued and supported by family members, institutions, and society at large.
Examples:

- *Conditioning* is complete when a person knows what to think, how to feel, what to do, how to act—and is unlikely to question that knowledge.

- A *conditioned* response to disapproval is to assume one is at fault.

Egocentricity (or ego): Literally, "I" as the center; the sense of a separate self resulting from the process of social conditioning; the subjective "I" that is in relation to the "objective" universe (the question of objectivity is addressed in the text).
Examples:

- Egocentricity perpetuates the belief that one's survival must be assured, no matter what the cost to others.

- Fear always arises from egocentricity.

- Egocentric is often used to modify conditioning.

- Egocentric conditioning produces the feeling that "I" is alone.

(In the way we use language here, saying "'I' is . . ." is a way of indicating that the "I" is an illusory viewpoint rather than the center of the universe that it believes itself to be.)

Suffering: The experience of being caught in the illusory world of separateness. Suffering can range from mild discomfort to abject misery; sometimes it is defined as dissatisfaction, in the broadest sense.

Examples:

- After practicing meditation for several months, Tom realized that even when things seemed to be going well, he experienced a constant if subtle level of suffering.

- This practice enables us to free ourselves from the world of suffering.

Subpersonality: An aspect of the illusory separate self, a persona, one of many such aspects that make up the personality. Subpersonalities are split off from the primary identity as a child encounters obstacles and is conditioned to deal with them in socially approved ways.

Examples:

- Johnny was afraid of the dark as a child, and as a result, he developed a superhero *subpersonality* who is afraid of nothing.

- Through the day, we move through numerous *subpersonalities*, without necessarily being aware of how appropriate each one is to the actual situation we are in.

Center: The present moment, here and now; the experience of being fully with what is. When we are centered, there is a sense of ease, completeness, belonging, well-being, a larger perspective in which the illusion of separateness is dispelled.

Examples:

- When Bob and Sally stepped back from their roles as adversaries and into *center*, they could each see alternative solutions for their shared problem.

- At *center*, there is nothing wrong.

Disidentification: The movement out of a subpersonality into center.
Examples:

- *Disidentification* involves taking a step back, seeing what part of our conditioning we are identified with, and choosing to be present instead.

- While driving to work, Janet suddenly *disidentified* from the "good daughter" image and became aware of how much effort that role required.

- Disidentification can also be the movement from one identity into another.

- Rick is "just one of the guys" as long as happy hour lasts, then he goes home, *disidentifies*, and assumes the role of "Mr. Domestic."

Projection: Attributing to others qualities in oneself (usually qualities that are not recognized or are difficult to acknowledge).
Examples:

- A person whose conditioning includes intense concern about a given subject—tidiness, punctuality, looks, money—is likely to *project* that other people make judgments based on the same degree of concern.

* In awareness practice, it is important to become aware of one's *projections*.

Some of the terms you will find in this book are familiar from psychology. Our use of those terms is likely to be different, in subtle but profoundly important ways. I would encourage you to pay close attention to those differences rather than assuming that you already know the meaning of such words. If you encounter terms or usages that you do not understand, keep reading, with an eye on allowing yourself to discover the experience *within* that the words point to. This in itself is a most helpful approach as we undertake this journey into awareness.

Two Possibilities

People live in one of two worlds. The first of these is ordinary reality, which consists almost entirely of an idea of how things should be, based on an imaginary past and future. The second world is the present moment of oneness with everything that *is*.

The ordinary reality is illusory. It is created through the process we call egocentric conditioning, by which we come to experience ourselves as separate from everything else. Egocentric conditioning is all that stands between you and what you are seeking.

Most of us live most of our lives within the conditioned reality of egocentricity. That means that, at any given moment, we are suffering to some degree from a belief that life is not as it should be, that there is something wrong. From that sense arise fear, worry, insecurity, resentment, criticism of others, self-criticism, tension, boredom, indulgence, guilt, blame, shame, confusion, and all other forms of misery and dissatisfaction.

In rare moments, we are present, here and now, not identified with an egocentric, conditioned, illusory belief in a separate self, but experiencing the ease, well-being, sufficiency, openness, acceptance, expansiveness, compassion, and even joy of nonseparateness. Such experiences tend to be brief; through tiny gaps in the near-constant barrage of messages from egocentricity, we glimpse the world in which nothing is wrong.

The awareness practice presented in this book enables us to learn which of these realities we are inhabiting, and how to move from one to the other.

※　　※　　※

It is not possible to stop suffering from *within* the world of suffering. Imagine this: You walk from the light into a dark house, down a dark hall, into a room with no windows or other sources of light, and you stand in the middle of it, ranting and raving about the darkness, hating the dark and yourself for being in it, despairing that it will never be different, wondering what's wrong with you for being there, and trying to figure out what to do. That is a pretty good image of what it's like to live in egocentric conditioning. Now, picture walking out of that room, down the hall, out of the house, and into the light. That is a pretty good image of the freedom that comes with awareness practice. We can walk out of that dark room anytime we choose.

Leaving that room is the choice we must make if we wish to end suffering—and it is imperative that we realize that choice is available only in the light. That is why we meditate. (Actually, we meditate not so much to enable us to walk out of that room into the light, but so that we can learn to recognize that we are in the room and eventually not go unconscious and walk into that house in the first place—but such distinctions are down the road a bit.)

The process we will work with here is extraordinarily subtle. I am going to ask you to learn to question your every assumption, everything you think you know. Your "koan" (a spiritual riddle, in the Zen tradition, that cannot be answered intellectually) is "Do I know that?" When, through a burst of intuitive knowing, you have successfully answered that koan, the next one will be, "How do I know that?"

Through this process, we learn to approach every moment of life without assumption, to cultivate a completely fresh awareness. If I hear a voice in my head say, "I'm not an artist," rather than experiencing a reaction to that statement and assuming that the reaction means the statement is true—because the voice has always said that and I have always believed it—I am going to question that voice. I will ask myself questions designed to enable me to examine the situation more carefully. "Is that true? How do I know that's true? What if it's not true? What does it mean if it *is* true? What would it mean if it weren't true? How did I get this information? Who is defining the terms? Who is setting the standards? How can I test this?"

The mind that asks these questions is open, inquiring, curious, alive, and free. Our purpose here is to bring conscious awareness to our moment-by-moment experience in order to see through and beyond the ways in which we have been conditioned, and to step free of what it is that causes us to suffer.

An Issue to Work With

Let's begin by selecting something you want to change in your life. Think of a problem you're currently having, a way in which you wish you were different, a circumstance that you can't seem to get out of, a behavior that is not leading you where you want to go, an orientation to life that is getting in your way, or something you've been trying to let go of but just can't seem to turn loose. What you're looking for is a quality or a behavior or an attitude or a habit. Choose something that has been around for a good while, something you've been working on, something you're familiar with and continue to be dissatisfied about.

Give yourself as much time as you need to identify the issue. This will be an issue that you use to practice awareness with as you go through this book. Pick just one issue. You will be learning a process that you can apply to any situation, but focusing on a single small issue in these exercises will make it easier to grasp each step as you untangle the problem.

Go over the issue in your mind as thoroughly as you can. See yourself as you are when you are in the throes of this situation. Take your time. It would be most helpful if you write down an overview of the problem or verbalize it into a tape recorder.

Personal Survey on Change

When you have completed your overview, carefully and thoroughly answer these questions:

- What would you like to *do* or *have* or *be* or *get* that is different? (In other words, what is the problem? What exactly would you like to change?)

- What makes this a problem? Is it that you don't like it, or that others don't like it? How do you know it is a problem?

- How long has this been an issue in your life?

- Is there anyone else involved?

- What have you done about this issue in the past?

- How has what you have done affected the problem? What has worked? What has not worked?

- What would it mean for you to change this? How would you be different? How would your life be different? How would you/your life be better? Worse?

- What stops you from having what you want?

Before going any further, I want to ask you to turn your attention to a subtle but crucially important point. When answering questions like these, it is very likely that your conditioning will immediately come into play—in ways that will prevent you from gaining anything from the exercise and keep you from making any changes.

First of all, conditioning may manifest as resistance. If you find yourself suddenly realizing that you have more important things to do than this exercise, or thinking that this is silly and probably won't work, or discovering that the issue you chose to work with really is not a problem after all, you just might want to consider that those are common forms of unconscious resistance to change.

Conditioning also manifests in less obvious ways. For instance, let's say I realize that I said something insensitive to a friend. Simply appreciating that insight will enable me to bring clearer awareness to future interactions with my friend, and thus, be more sensitive in that relationship. But my conditioning may be to respond to that insight with something such as, "See what kind of person you are? You are cruel and hateful. You'd better watch out or you won't have any friends at all." The implication is that without conditioning to monitor, control, and punish my behavior, I will be a horrible person. In fact, it can be argued that conditioning is doing everything it can to prevent the insights that would free me from the conditioned survival responses that are causing (in this case) my insensitive behavior.

Becoming aware of how conditioning blocks change is so important that, at the risk of sounding repetitious, I am going to draw it to your attention at the end of each personal survey.

Remember: You are seeking greater awareness about this issue in order to better see the ways in which you have been conditioned. Your conditioning is not the same as your true self. Be careful not to allow your conditioning to use your awareness against you.

While doing this work, you will learn to see where you are, where you want to go, what you need to do to get from point to point, and most important of all, *what stops you.*

Now, I recognize that a lot of people don't want to do the work involved in learning these things. It's much more appealing to read a book, get some information, and congratulate yourself on your intellectual understanding. However, as most of us know from long experience, reading books does not change how we operate, and acquiring information does not develop a skill. You cannot learn ballet dancing from a book. You cannot learn to sing from a book. You cannot learn to swim from a book. You can fit information *about* those things into your conditioning, but until you actually begin practicing those pliés and singing those scales and swimming those strokes, you will have learned nothing truly new.

Only the moment-by-moment awareness practice that enables you to see through your social conditioning will allow you to be where you want to be. I will walk you through the process, and you can practice the various steps.

This is not an intellectual process. If you read the book but don't do the steps, nothing will happen for you. Then, awareness practice will be filed under "One more thing that doesn't work," and you will fail to notice that you never actually *did* it.

Keep in mind that everything is part of the process. As long as you don't quit, you are still participating. In fact, it can be argued that quitting can be part of the process, another step to explore, a detour rather than an end. One of my books is titled *How You Do Anything Is How You Do Everything*—which is true. If you really want to know how you are you, simply pay attention to everything, believe nothing, and don't take anything personally. Everything is a clue. Every resistance, every little bit of miserable conditioning, every cry of helpless victimization brings you a gift of clarity, wisdom, and compassion. Don't miss any of it.

Are you ready to begin?

Seeing into the Issue

To demonstrate how this process works, each chapter will provide questions for you to consider with respect to the issue you have chosen. The sample issue we will use is wanting to work for myself and not doing it. Substitute your own issue, and let's begin our exploration.

I want to [work for myself].

Working for myself feels like an important goal, but I never seem to make much progress in realizing it. When I mention it, people offer reasonable, concrete, even exciting suggestions for how I can make it happen. I need to have clear goals, they tell me. I need to be sure that this is an authentic ambition. I need to find support. I need to have a mentor. I need to be disciplined. I need to take certain steps each day. All these are excellent ideas for solving my problem. I can see exactly what I need to do to achieve my goal of working for myself.

But my immediate problem is this: *I don't do those things.* I don't act on the good advice of my friends. Day after day goes by without my taking any of the steps that I know I need to take in order to work for myself. I have made resolutions, called myself names, punished myself—and nothing changes. I feel completely frustrated, a failure. What can I do?

Often the answer to that question is, "Try harder. If at first you don't succeed, try, try again." But when you've tried and tried and tried, done everything you know how to do over and over, and still gotten nowhere, the thought of trying yet again just leaves you demoralized.

I would like to suggest looking in a completely different direction. Meanwhile, here are some questions for your consideration:

- Do you think you are the only person with this kind of difficulty?

- Have you ever known or heard of anyone who had an issue they could not seem to resolve? Is your problem worse than theirs?

- If you had a friend in this situation, what would you advise?

The next chapter is about going into, through, and beyond what stands between us and what we want.

CHAPTER TWO

ILLUSION:
Between Us and What We Want

A s we embark on this practice of awareness, it can be helpful to consider this: To move from where we are to where we want to be is a single step. Now, the difficulty is that that step takes us outside the illusion that we have always thought of as life, which can be a very threatening idea. But let me offer a different perspective.

Imagine the experience of a newborn infant. Imagine not being able to discriminate sights, sounds, smells, and sensation; not knowing what anything is or what anything means or how things go together; and having no idea who people are, or what is good, bad, right, wrong, helpful, or dangerous. Picture not only not knowing that you are *you*, but not even knowing that you *are* a you. Imagine that there is nothing "other," no one "else." Everything is one big, undifferentiated "this" with no "that": no separation, no spaces, no end of me and beginning of you—just "we." Everything is equal. Everything is the same. All is one. Now, think about your reality, and consider for a moment that everything you have experienced in your life since you were an infant—the entire universe as you know it—is a systematically conditioned program of beliefs and assumptions that you have been taught.

That, in fact, is what has happened to each of us. *Conditioning* is the term we use to refer to this process.

Conditioning is possible only because human beings have the unique ability to experience themselves as separate from life. It's possible for a human being to be physically in one reality and mentally in another. This ability is the wonder and the curse of humanity.

To understand this, we must go back to one of our most fundamental assumptions about life. The popular way of looking at birth is that a new life comes into being. But a baby is not a new life; it is a new *form*. Life *is*. Being *is*. It does not come and go; our perceptions come and go, and particular forms come and go. This is an extremely important point: It is this unexamined, false assumption that life begins and ends that perpetuates the illusion of a self that is separate from life. And that illusion is the origin of our suffering.

A baby is born out of life and into a context. Very soon, the interaction of the baby with its context begins a process of creating and maintaining the illusion of an individual identity that continues for most people until the dissolution of the body.

How the Illusion Is Created

A human being possesses the ability to remember and discriminate. This means that we can learn to see one thing as separate and distinct from another, and we can hold a picture of that thing in our mind or store that picture in our memory in order to apply it at another time. As soon as possible, a child is taught how to relate to the environment the family considers reality. (Currently there is an effort to begin the conditioning process in the womb by reading, talking, and playing music to the fetus.) Over and over, information is repeated to the baby: who a certain person is; what we call that person; what this object is; what that object is for; how we feel about this (ummmm, good!); how we feel about that (yuck, dirty!); and, through it all, unspoken information is transmitted about what all this *means*. The child is rewarded (with approval) for the right response, and punished (approval withheld) for the wrong response.

Regardless of the circumstances, the conditioning *process*, if not the *content*, develops along the same lines for all of us. The content, the particulars, vary. In one family, orderliness (or spontaneity or discipline or emotional expressiveness or whatever) is encouraged, while in another, it is scorned. In some families, one parent holds one view, and the other parent holds the opposite view. In some cases, a particular kind of behavior is encouraged in certain circumstances and not in others. The process, though—how conditioning is accomplished—is the same: *What is conducive to survival of the individual is adopted, and what threatens the survival of the individual is avoided.*

We must keep in mind that a child has no information other than that which is provided by the environment. A child lacks any social network or access to a larger perspective, and so has no chance to ask around. Many adults *believe* that children know how they are expected to behave, and even *accuse* children of knowing ("He does that because he knows it annoys me"), but children only have the information they have been given, directly or indirectly.

"Eat your vegetables; people are starving." What in the world does *that* mean? What message are we meant to derive from that? As a small child, I don't know that there are people other than the ones I've seen. I don't know that there are other countries. What is a country? I don't know what *starving* means. I don't know what eating my vegetables has to do with anything—with growth, with health, or with money. I've never not had food. I don't know what gratitude is, let alone that it might be associated with *getting* stuff. All I understand is the idea that not eating what's on your plate makes you a bad person in the eyes of the people around you. Eating everything is really important. (And many of us are still trying to meet that standard.) Here is the point to keep in mind: Children cannot allow their survival to rest with an unknown. If a message is not clear, the child learns to make up meaning from what the message sounds like or feels like or seems like.

This is why we cannot predict how a child will be affected by a particular circumstance. For instance, father's way of communicating his displeasure is to yell and wave his arms around. One child is terrified and spends a lifetime in dread of a man raising his voice. Another child responds by egging Dad on, and takes that pattern into the rest of life, pushing people until they yell. (As an aside, it's common to see parents threatening children who seem not to take the threats seriously. If threats of punishment are used to control the behavior of a small child, the parent is in a rough spot when the child learns that the parent can't or won't follow through on the threat. I remember thinking as a child, *What are they going to do, kill me?* From that moment on, I only followed those rules I chose to adhere to.)

❈   ❈   ❈

I use examples, metaphors, and analogies to attempt to communicate the very difficult notion of social conditioning. Often people hear the example and respond with something such as, "Oh, that never happened to me," and the conclusion they reach is that *they must not have been conditioned.* No, no, no. We all have been conditioned, and we are all living out that conditioning.

Here is the difficulty as I see it: Finding differences serves egocentricity in a way that finding similarities does not. Therefore, we are always conditioned to see the differences between everything and to compare. It is considered a mark of intelligence to be able to perceive the most subtle differences. In some situations, this is useful, but in general, certainly in human relations, it is a huge cause of suffering. If people focused on the similarities between people, war would be impossible. Instead, people focus on relatively small differences and then hate and kill one another over those differences. *They* speak a different language. *They* have a different skin color. *They* worship a different God. *They* worship God in a different way. *They* believe something we don't believe. These are small differences when we consider that all people have language, all people have skin, most people worship, and everyone on Earth believes different things (even those who want to believe that they share the same beliefs as those around them).

Egocentricity has its life in being other, different, and separate. It thrives on struggle, conflict, and strife. Egocentricity wants to find the point of disagreement in everything. So, when an example is given—Jill's mother, always wishing she could have been a nightclub singer, forced Jill to take singing lessons, with the result that now Jill will barely speak—see if you can avoid the conditioned temptation to think, *Wow, my mom never made me take anything. Guess this doesn't apply to me.* Instead, look to see what *did* happen in your youth. Did you wish you could have lessons, but your family couldn't afford them? Did you have lessons and love them? What were you forced to do? Can you see how being forced to do something in childhood has caused you to avoid it in adulthood? Do you find yourself holding beliefs about the value of teaching children certain skills whether or not the child wants to participate? Do parents have the right to force children? Are there things you were not required to do that you now *regret* not being able to do?

There are no absolutely correct answers to these questions. However, each answer will reveal our conditioning. That is, every reaction we have can tell us something about ourselves if we pay attention. Please keep in mind that I am not saying that parents are doing anything wrong. Social conditioning is something that each of us has received and each of us continues to do to ourselves, to one another, and to all children. There is no fault or blame. Until we see where we are, there is no hope of going anywhere else.

How the Illusion Is Transmitted

In discussions of this perspective on social conditioning, parents tend to become alarmed and want to know how they can avoid doing to their children what was done to them. My response is that our children learn *who we are*, not what we try to teach them. The old expression, "Do as I say, not as I do," is necessary precisely because reality is the very opposite. Children do as we *do*, not as we *say*. As long as our way of being is dictated by the social conditioning we received, we will automatically pass that same conditioning along to our children, like an infectious disease. The only way we can cease to transmit the harmful aspects of our own early conditioning is to recognize it in ourselves and consciously let it go.

A father told me about observing his three-year-old son in a fit of frustration. The child had a look of such disgusted impatience on his face that the father was alarmed. It was not a look that anyone would wish to see on an innocent young face. There was nothing that the father could do except attempt to support the boy in his endeavors, and dissuade him from what appeared to be a very harsh judgment of himself, but the incident troubled the father nonetheless. A few weeks later, the father was in his own fit of frustration, and in one of those moments of insight for which we can be grateful, he *felt* his face twisted into the same disgusted impatience he had seen on his little boy. The child, watching his father to see how a human being operates, had mimicked his father's frustration just as he might imitate his father's walk, speech, or way of dressing.

Similarly, when my daughter was six years old, I became

aware that she had a slightly arrogant, sarcastic tone to her way of speaking that was not at all attractive in such a small child. As with the father in the preceding story, I saw in a flash of intuitive understanding that my daughter talked the way she heard her mother talk—and I realized that that manner of speech was not attractive in me either. Fortunately, she soon grew out of it. Her mother is making progress.

We fail to realize that children miss nothing. Before the process of social conditioning, the child naturally looks inward for information—seeing the world with fresh, clear eyes that have not yet been taught to see only certain things in certain ways and not to see other things at all. Like little sponges, they take in everything, exactly as is, unfiltered. Children don't play by our conditioned rules of it not being acceptable to see certain things and so pretending not to. When a child's comments are not threatening to adult reality, they are seen as cute and charming. When, however, those comments require the adult to glimpse, consciously or unconsciously, an unconditioned reality behind the conditioned reality, the child will elicit disapproval, or even rejection.

How the Illusion Is Maintained

Each person in a parental role (mother/father/aunt/uncle/grandparent/foster parent) makes this sort of agreement with a child: *I am your caregiver, and if you please me, if you are the way I want you to be, if you do what I say (to validate my worldview), I will love you and give you everything you need, or at the very least, keep you alive.* In an attempt to keep up their end of the bargain—and please the person in whose hands survival rests—children learn to turn away from themselves and choose what the caregiver says over their own experience. The child agrees: *If you will care for me and see that my needs are met, I will give you authority over my life.*

For example, as your mother, I tell you not to lie. Yet when you point out how fat Aunt Ethel is, I respond in horror and let you know that there is something really wrong with you for saying such a thing. At every family gathering Uncle Ed passes out in his soup, reeking of whiskey, and you're told he's not feeling well. When you learn to say, as he lands in the soup, that Uncle Ed is not feeling well, you get a lot of acceptance. In the same way, little Joey learns that he doesn't like dolls, and little Jill learns to shriek when Joey pulls a frog out of his pocket—and the whole family breathes a collective sigh of relief. Social conditioning is firmly in place, and all is right with the world.

Again and again, as children, we receive information telling us that those around us are involved in a complicated "arrangement" and that we need to figure out what to do and not to do, what to say and not to say, how to be and not to be within that arrangement, without letting on that we are aware of it. As children, we each made that agreement to please an external authority who would meet all our needs—and for each of us it was a bad deal. Why? Because regardless of how loving and committed and well intentioned they may be, no person can meet the essential needs of another. No one can replace the authentic self of someone else. Once we leave ourselves, we are bound to suffer, until we return to our own authenticity.

When the conditioning process has been completed, around the age of seven or eight (according, I'm told, to both modern psychology and traditional Roman Catholic thinking), we have learned to refer to the world of social rules for information rather than referring to ourselves in the unconditioned reality of the present moment. We no longer look to our body and emotions and intuition to tell us how to respond; we look to what we've been conditioned to believe we *should* do. What have I been told? What should I feel? What is the right way to behave under these circumstances? What is the right answer?

Postures

Our beliefs, assumptions, opinions, standards, concepts, and judgments are what we call "postures." These postures define us and distinguish us from others.

Because we believe so strongly in the "truth" of our opinions, and because we so desperately cling to the notion that there is a "right" answer, we constantly look toward the people who *know*, the authorities, the ones with the right information. We forget— we have been taught and are encouraged to forget—that no one *knows* anything. What we think of as the givens of life are all fabrications of our conditioned minds. It all seems logical, it makes us feel more secure, and we believe it. We convince ourselves and one another. We dislike, reject, punish, and sometimes kill those who do not agree. Often we learn later that there is new information, a new opinion, a better idea, a truer belief, and we begin the process of adjusting to the new reality. It doesn't seem to bother people that we are convinced and fervently believe something that turns out to be false; it's the *process* of believing that seems to be essential. Believing something makes people feel secure, even when they know, deep down, that it is not true.

Our postures may serve the aims of society, but they do not serve our purpose here. We are attempting to bring conscious awareness to our moment-by-moment experience. To judge what we see as good or bad derails our efforts to see *what is*. If what I see is viewed as unacceptable, the result is that I learn *not* to see what is so, in a misguided attempt to make myself believe I am the way I've been taught I should be. But lying to myself does not change the way I am. Lying to myself is lying to myself, and if I'm fooling myself, I'm compounding the problem.

Meaning

Clinging to our beliefs about what things mean is how we avoid seeing that those meanings aren't true. Most of us are terrified of questioning the validity of those meanings, because that involves going against our internal programming, which we think keeps us safe. But not examining the hidden meanings prevents us from addressing the issues in our lives that cause us to suffer.

For instance, I think that if I take more than is considered my share, I might be seen as selfish, and being selfish *means* I am a bad person. But does it? Taking "more than my share" doesn't *mean* anything except that I am a person who on this occasion took more than what was considered (by someone) "my share."

Doing acts identified as "kind" does not make you a good person; it does not even mean you are kind. Doing kind acts makes you a person who is currently doing what someone has labeled "kind acts." Having a lot of money does not make you greedy; you are simply a person who has a lot of money. Yelling at the kids does not make you a bad parent, it makes you a parent who is yelling at the kids.

When we can separate behaviors from all the "meanings" that define a person, we can sort them into groups and address each for what it is, like sorting the socks. I cannot look with fresh eyes at my relationship with money as long as I am busy either defending myself against, or identifying myself with, a label of "greedy." I cannot have an uncluttered view into my relationship with food as long as I see myself as an undisciplined, indulgent pig. I will not be able to get past the label long enough to be able to find any clarity about the issue.

This is an extremely subtle and enormously important point. What would the issues of your life look like if none of them *meant* anything?

I am not saying that the issues are unimportant. I am not suggesting that they should be ignored. I am simply suggesting that an issue will never be seen for what it is, and the solution to the problem will never be apparent, as long as we are stuck focusing on the erroneous and irrelevant baggage of meaning that has gotten attached to it.

A common analogy to this process can be found in our government. A bill is introduced for consideration by legislators. Certain interests want the bill to become law, and to make sure that will happen, they are willing to overlook a lot that they don't agree with. That opens the door for others to attach irrelevant pieces of legislation to it that *they* want, with the result being that the whole bundle, irrelevancies and all, is passed into law. Attaching meaning works in a similar way in our lives. Social conditioning involves tagging all sorts of irrelevant meanings onto behavior. The resulting bundle of patterned, programmed thoughts, feelings, and actions is a conditioned human being.

The Social Program

In fact, everything in the world of conditioning is made up. We must be programmed to believe what we believe, because otherwise we would never conclude, for example, that people are more or less important based on their income, looks, religion, skin color, sexual orientation, education, or occupation. To a young child, those are irrelevancies. Babies clearly know and express what is important to them: being in a congenial temperature, with full tummies and dry clothes. If the body is comfortable, everything is fine. If the body is not comfortable, they let us know. As long as comfort is provided, they are perfectly all right; they have no opinions about the "value" of the provider of that comfort. All of the information about comparative importance and worth, better and worse, every basis for judgment—which supports the illusion of being separate that is the cause of our suffering—is added slowly, moment by moment, as the child grows.

If we can grasp that the world we have been taught to see is made up, and grasp that we have been socially engineered to fit into it and perpetuate it, why can't we just accept that and turn to what is real? Because to most people, allowing that perception to slip in would be as threatening as the earth dropping out from under us, leaving us to fall helplessly through space.

What is there to hold on to if what we have been taught to believe is not the truth? What do we believe? What can we trust? What is going to happen to us? We wouldn't know who to be, what to do, or how to act. Without our conditioned reality to tell us what's what, the world would be in chaos and we would be out of control. Even when there is that nagging suspicion that the whole thing is made up, people would rather deny that possibility and believe what is not real than face the anxiety and insecurity of admitting that nobody knows.

Here is something I received from someone struggling with selfishness, selflessness, and judgment. As you read this, see if you can become aware of socially conditioned patterns within yourself that are similar to or different from Charlotte's.

CHARLOTTE

I'm jealous of friends and acquaintances who (seemingly) receive love and money unconditionally from their families without having given or sacrificed for them I feel I have given and have not received. This is especially so in my having taken care of elderly neighbors whose grown children did not help when it was needed. I see the children as selfish (in not taking time to visit their parents). I was not selfish. I was good. I did what they should have done.

I know I am judging. But I don't understand how my seeing their lack of care (selfishness, which is provable in

a reality check) makes me selfish. Because I see selfish-
ness doesn't mean I am selfish, does it? To recognize it
means I know that behavior. So I own it, saying I, too,
have been selfish, am selfish sometimes. So we are alike.
Seeing that, I should feel compassion for them and not
judge them.

But I'm jealous, and I'm unhappy about that. I don't
approve of being jealous. I feel small. I'm angry that I
cared for their parents, then they come along and never
say even a thank you, inherit all the money and stuff, and
go on their way. It's not the money that bothers me, I
don't think. It's that I sacrificed (so maybe I didn't care
for them in my heart?); and now I feel deprived, jealous,
and miserable.

I get jealous over other deprivation issues: people
with families, grandchildren, good health, money, confi-
dence. It's the jealousy I want to get rid of in my life. It's
daily, and I suffer with it. Then I hear I should just let go
of this jealousy.

So, where am I? Am I missing the point?

The part of us that holds a conditioned belief is not going to
give it up willingly. A part—in this case the part of you that holds
beliefs about selfishness, about who is and who isn't selfish,
about what does and does not constitute selfish behavior—will
cling to an identification with your conditioning—not in *spite* of
the suffering created by those beliefs, but *because* of the suffering created by those beliefs. This is a perfect example of the
world of conditioned illusion, or delusion. The stage is set: Life
is this way, people should be this way, people who are the way
they should be are good and will be rewarded, people who are not
the way they should be are bad and will be punished. It may

sound familiar—but none of it was ever true.

"I don't understand how my seeing their lack of care (self-ishness, which is provable in a reality check) makes me selfish." Ah, the subtleties. First of all, was there a reality check? Consulting our conditioned views for verification of our conditioned views and getting a verification is not a reality check. The critical piece we have to grasp is that our conditioned view of the world is simply our conditioned view of the world. We can find others whose views are the same, but that just means that our conditioning is the same; it doesn't mean that we're right or that our view is "true."

"I see a person as selfish." Well, where does that idea come from? It comes from my conditioned standard of selfishness. That person's behavior doesn't meet my standard. That's all.

Now, here is the kicker. The reason that this is such an issue for me (speaking as the person who is focused on selfishness) is that all of my life I've been twisting myself into knots, trying not to act out of my "selfish" impulses. If I didn't have such strong prohibitions against certain behaviors, I would be acting *exactly* as these other people are—maybe more so. But I cannot. I am simply not allowed, and, therefore, I cannot stand it when they are allowed to act the way I would act but cannot. Of course I feel jealous. They are getting to have what I am not allowed to have.

Seeking Safety Through Punishment

Even though as individuals we may chafe against the external controls of society, the belief that punishment makes people behave is so strong that the idea of removing it is intolerable. We tell ourselves that we are afraid of what "they" might do if they weren't being controlled. A closer look, however, will show us that this is pure projection—we are afraid of being uncontrolled ourselves.

We have been deeply conditioned to believe that punishment is what makes people good and keeps them that way. From childhood on, we have been taught that left to ourselves, without someone to watch over us and punish us, we will be bad. This is small-child thinking, but most people still operate from it. With the completion of social conditioning, each individual is charged with doing their own watching, monitoring, and punishing. Guilt is good, says social conditioning. Without it, you would be selfish, lazy, and indulgent. You would do bad things, and without feeling guilty, there would be nothing to stop you.

When questioned about these beliefs, people often try to hide behind the old idea that children need to be conditioned for their own safety. Consider this: A child picks up an expensive object that she has been told not to pick up. "Put that down right now! Shame on you. You're a bad girl." Sound familiar? There may be no danger at all to the child—the danger is to the adult. The adult is protecting himself *and* a worldview. The adult has projected all sorts of meaning and value onto the object and does not want to lose that object, and by extension, that value and meaning. Is the child bad for picking it up? Should she be ashamed? Is there anything the matter with her? Of course not, but it is an essential, unconscious message from the adult: "Do as I tell you, because when you look only to yourself, you get it wrong, and you do bad and shameful things."

I can hear someone saying, "But what about physical safety? Should we let our children just run into the street in front of cars?" Obviously not. What is it about not looking before going into the street that makes a child bad? It is true that a child is not able to think ahead, not able to comprehend danger, injury, or death, and therefore must be protected. But making children feel that they are bad because they cannot comprehend complex ideas such as danger, injury, and death seems flawed. The child is ignorant of a larger picture, but not *bad*.

A Parallel Reality and the Land of "Should"

As stated earlier, with our ability to discriminate and remember, human beings are able to appear to live in two worlds at once. The difficulty with this sleight of hand is that people don't realize that they are merging what is real with what is imaginary. A simple example: I have decided to accompany my husband to a business conference so we can have some time together without the kids. Instead of the romantic interlude I have imagined, I am abandoned in a strange city while he schmoozes with the guys. I wail, "I should have known this wouldn't work. I should never have come on this trip. I should have stayed home and painted the kitchen."

How can I make myself so miserable? Because I have the ability to remember and discriminate. I imagine the time that I want to spend with my partner. I can see it so vividly in my mind that I fail to notice that it is absolute fiction, all made up, and does not exist anywhere except in my mind. Then I get attached to that illusion. In my mind, it is real, and there is no room for anything else. I go over the dream, fill in the details, embellish it—we'll go there, I'll wear this, he'll say that, and we'll be so happy together. I don't need to tell him any of it because I assume he is sharing my reality. Alas, he has been doing the same process, except that in *his* version, *he* is the star. He'll meet so-and-so and say such-and-such, and they'll have a drink and make a deal. . . .

Once the social conditioning process is complete, we live almost exclusively in the parallel reality of how things *should* be. Life as it actually is often appears to be an annoying, unfair interruption of our pursuit of life. In life as it should be, I get what I want, people do what I want, things are easy, lights are green, traffic flows smoothly, people are polite and helpful, what I want to buy is on sale, things never break, my loved ones are happy and well and successful and adore me, and I am attractive and financially secure forever. How do I know that's how life should be? It's so obvious! I *see* it—when something goes "wrong," I can see how it should have been. How do I know I believe that's how life should be? I can tell by how upset I am when life isn't that way.

Attempted Escape (an aside)

Many of us reached a point in adolescence when we made a last-ditch effort not to succumb to what we clearly saw as the craziness of the adult world. Adults were phony, hypocritical, deluded, and out of touch with reality. "I'm not going to be like that!" we asserted. By that time we were already conditioned. Our reaction to what we saw around us was merely to go in the opposite direction, to the other side of the duality. "If adults value tidiness, I'll be a slob," says the rebellious adolescent. "If they think healthy eating is important, I'll eat junk. They think drugs are dangerous, so I will take drugs. They think I should work toward the future they value, so I will do the opposite."

Individuals caught on this seesaw do not see that they are not free at all—they are just as trapped, just as deluded as adults. The adult says yes, the adolescent says no, and they are stuck at opposite ends of the same continuum. Most of us have passed the point where rebelling loses its charm, whereupon we decided that the adult world of conditioned reality is what we want after all. As if that were a choice. . . .

There is no freedom in doing the opposite. Freedom lies in moving easily along the whole continuum, as appropriate—and that choice is possible only when we have stepped out of the illusion altogether.

Dualism

The structure of our illusory, conditioned reality is maintained by dualism. As we grow in conditioning, we are taught an overwhelming list of qualities and characteristics that are desirable and that we must exemplify if we are to be good, bright, and acceptable (which may explain why so many people feel overwhelmed by life). We are taught an equal and opposite list of qualities and characteristics that are undesirable and that we must never be or do because then we would be bad, wrong, and unacceptable.

You must always be:	You must never be:
strong	weak
good	bad
right	wrong
kind	unkind
selfless	selfish
smart	stupid
successful	a failure

We could go on filling in pairs indefinitely. Life consists of good/bad, right/wrong, night/day, black/white, us/them, me/you. The cruelty of this is that we are not all given the same list; we are not taught the relationship between the two sides; we are not taught *how*. How do you get to success? How do you know when the goal has been achieved? How long does the success last? How do you relate to its coming to an end? How does success relate to failure? How do you handle failure?

The physical world we live in is not dualistic, it is a continuum. Night does not at some point stop being night and suddenly become a separate, distinct, other thing called day. They are each an aspect of one thing. We live our lives in day-nights.

Unfortunately, most of us have been conditioned to cling to

each side of a continuum while attempting to push away the other. Day is positive, night is negative. In fact, just as there is no night without day, and no day without night, there can be no good without bad, no right without wrong, no me without you, no us without them, no this without that. Yet we live our lives on these seesaws of false dichotomy, believing we should be able to have one side without the other.

Our lives consist of a constant monitoring of our position and movement along countless continuums. The monitoring is done by comparing. Each interaction, each exchange, each registering of information on any level is an experience of comparison. How am I doing? How did that sound? How did he take that? How do I look? What was her reaction? Did I do that well? Was that enough? Too much? Each comparison addresses the unasked question from our childhood conditioning: "Am I surviving?"

The irony is that the question of survival is asked by conditioning of conditioning about conditioning. The only survival being monitored is the survival of conditioning. The survival may not, and usually does not, have anything to do with the actual well-being of the individual. For example, people can have serious accidents because they are unwilling to admit that they need glasses. People allow their closest relationships to deteriorate because they refuse to wear hearing aids. I've even heard of cases in which someone with food stuck in their airway choked to death in a rest room rather than endure the embarrassment of causing a scene in a restaurant.

The Difficulty

When discussing social conditioning, people often want to idealize past cultures, hoping that those other people somehow managed to elude our fate. I see no evidence that any such exemption ever existed. All peoples, all societies, and all cultures have used some form of social conditioning to regulate the behavior of citizens. Could it be otherwise? Of course—if that were what people wanted. But people do *not* want it.

The reason we cannot see through this illusion created by social conditioning—the illusion I would suggest is the root cause of all human suffering—is that we are trying to comprehend that which contains us. As Albert Einstein put it, we are attempting to "solve a problem with the same mind that created it," and that cannot be done. I cannot use a conditioned mind to see my conditioned mind. I have to be "outside" the conditioning to gain a perspective from which to view it.

To get a taste of being outside our conditioning, try to imagine the following:

What would your world be like if you were living in China 500 years ago? Imagine the world of a female person rather than a male. Imagine the differences between the lives of a wealthy person and a poor person.

What would it be like to live in an African village 300 years ago? Imagine being old and left behind by the slave traders.

Picture being an unwed mother in the world of Charles Dickens.

Picture being under suspicion for heresy in the days of the Inquisition.

Imagine being born blind or unable to walk or speak.

Imagine living before germs were identified. Disease kills people every day, but no one knows how or why; explanations range from witchcraft to the wrath of God. Many women die during or shortly after childbirth, and infants die in large numbers.

Now, how many of the issues currently in your life would be issues in those times and under those circumstances? If you could step outside your specific conditioning, would you consider your "problems" problems? Would you have the same relationships with family and friends? Would you approach your future in the same way? Would you have the same expectations about life?

Personal Survey on Beliefs and Assumptions

Have you ever wondered which of our current beliefs and assumptions about life might be just as baseless as notions from other times and places that we scoff at as "primitive"? The following questions may reveal unconsciously held, culturally supported but not necessarily true ideas that operate in our lives every day.

- When you get what you want, do you think you're being rewarded for good behavior?

- If you have a disappointment, do you try to figure out what you did wrong to deserve it?

- Do you believe that if you pay close enough attention, you can control what happens to you?

- When people get sick, do you wonder what they did to cause their illness?

Remember: *When considering these questions, you are seeking to better see the ways in which you have been conditioned. Seeing your own conditioning is not the same as judging yourself. Please do not allow conditioning to use your growing awareness against you.*

The World of Opposites

The illusory dualistic world is often referred to in Eastern philosophy as "the world of opposites." This is commonly understood to mean black/white, good/bad, us/them, and should/ shouldn't. After looking for some time at this whole process of creating an artificial reality, I have come to the conclusion that the world of opposites actually refers not only to dualism, but to the fact that so many things are the opposite of what we've been taught to believe.

For example, contrary to what we've been told, dissatisfaction does not lead to satisfaction; it leads to dissatisfaction. Disliking something does not move you toward something that you will like; it trains you to dislike. Wanting something does not result in getting what you want; wanting results in a habit of wanting. Hating something does not make it go away; it causes it to continue. Trying to change keeps things the same. Trying to improve keeps you unacceptable.

How is this so? Because one process does not lead to another. It is not true—it is, in fact, false—that doing one thing will result in another, opposite outcome. War does not result in peace. Treating a disease does not create health. Having a lot of money does not lead to happiness.

The reality a person exists in is created and maintained by the focus of that person's attention. What you place your attention on determines the quality of your life.

This is why we practice awareness. If we don't know what we are attending to, if we don't know what reality we are keeping in place through the focus of our attention, we are doomed to continue doing the same things we've always done while hoping for a different outcome.

The situation described below illustrates how we are unwittingly caught in repeated behaviors over which we seem to have no control.

SERIAL VICTIM

Paul related an amazing story about his relationships with women. He had been married three times, and each time his wife had left him for another man. Before each of the wives left with a new partner, she'd had other affairs. In between the marriages, Paul had had girl-friends, each of whom he had caught in an affair. "Have you ever been involved with a woman who was faithful to you?" I asked. "Never," he replied, with just a touch of what might have been pride. He seemed so calm about the whole thing. "Well, Paul," I asked him," how are you managing to do that?" It was his turn to be amazed—it had never occurred to him that he might be playing some part in this pattern.

❋ ❋ ❋

Until we realize that we can take responsibility, we have no choice but to be a victim. Even if, like Paul, we make a "good sport" identity out of suffering wrongs perpetrated by others, we are still in the victim role. As we pay closer attention, we realize that, difficult as it may be to see initially, we always have choice in our life experience.

That realization is empowering. If life is simply an external force that acts upon me, and I have no choice but to react as I do, unless I'm really lucky, life will be hard and painful much of the time. If I realize that I can learn to see what is going on, make the connections and understand how things work, and from that greater understanding create different responses, life gets much easier and more interesting.

Using an example of a more common concern, let's say that I hate my overweight body. I believe that if I stop hating my fat and my deplorable eating habits, before long I will weigh a ton. All of my attention is directed to how fat I am, how much I eat, how incapable I am of stopping myself, and how much punishment I deserve for being this way. I don't realize that I am keeping the cycle in place through the constancy of my attention. I am so focused on how I believe I am that there is no room for any other possibility. In 12-step programs, this process is defined as *insanity*—doing the same thing over and over, hoping for a different outcome. Here's a similar account.

KAREN

I'm struggling with bulimia. I feel guilty about it and powerless to stop it. It takes up a lot of my time and money. I can't get into better physical shape, I can't lose weight, and my self-esteem is adversely affected. Other people are thoroughly disgusted by my condition. It is more acceptable to be an alcoholic, sex addict, or wife beater—anything short of being a murderer. People are so offended and bewildered by this behavior that I have to keep it secret.

❋   ❋   ❋

Not *What*, But *How*

My teacher introduced me to the notion that "it's not *what*, it's *how*." When I first heard that phrase, it had about as much meaning as if he had said, "It's not green dogs, it's pink kangaroos." At least I would have realized immediately that I had no way to relate to that sentence, but it seemed as if I should be able to understand those five simple words that he repeated so often. He sometimes mentioned that people would say to him partway through a conversation, "I understand every word you're saying, but I don't have any idea what you're talking about." That was my experience exactly.

During that period of my training, I was assisting one of the other monks in offering workshops in the larger community.

We would travel to various cities and lead workshops on the structures and processes we were attempting to bring into awareness: postures (beliefs and assumptions), projection, subpersonalities, disidentification, and centering. We would teach people how to sit in meditation, and offer support for their fledgling forays into awareness practice.

When I returned to the monastery after a workshop, my teacher would assist me in exploring the ins and outs of the interactions with the participants. In that way, he helped me see a larger perspective than the one that was currently available to me. I didn't realize it at the time, but he was guiding me to step back from each limited view and see a broader picture. We would be talking, and he would say, "Well, you know, it's not *what*, it's *how*," and my brain would come to a screeching halt. *What does that mean?* Then he would go on with what he was saying, and I would relax. Finally, I realized that if that sentence, "It's not *what*, it's *how*" appeared in every conversation, it must be important.

Eventually, I got to the point where I could tell when he was going to say it. I didn't know why it would occur at that particular point, but I knew that was the place for it, and I began to anticipate the announcement: Here it comes—he's going to say, "Well, you know, it's not *what*, it's *how*."

I can remember the moment when the lights came on. I was telling him about learning (from a mutual friend) that a woman I had known for years hated me. I was shocked. As I went on about how I just couldn't believe it was possible, my teacher said to me, "Who did she hate before you?" In a blinding flash, I saw it all: She had been actively hating one person or another forever. As the recognition dawned, he smiled and said, "Well, you know, it's not *what*, it's *how*"—and I *did* know. Yes! I was the *what*, and her process of hating people was the *how*.

To me, the heartbreaking sadness inherent in our unconscious acceptance of our conditioning is that instead of questioning the original premise in the way we've been taught to approach life, we assume that every problem is with *ourselves*. Then we turn to self-hate as the way of dealing with it, we blame and punish ourselves, and we pass the same process of suffering on to our children.

Seeing into the Issue by Noticing the Process

With this framework in mind, let's turn to the problem you identified as something in your life that you wish to change. Here is the first question to ask when beginning to explore the issue you have chosen to work with:

How do I not [work for myself]? (Substitute your own issue.)

It is not true that not working for myself is "just how it is." Not working for myself is not some external turn of events that has dropped into my life and I am now helpless in the face of it. Not working for myself does not happen by accident. Not working for myself is something I am *doing*. It is not a piece of *content*—a "what" as we're fond of calling it—such as a car payment or an annoying co-worker, but a process. Every time I don't do what is necessary to work for myself, I go through the same process to get to that same place.

That process is a complex system of sensations in one's body, beliefs, conditioning, emotional reactions, and behavior patterns.

To decide that I'm not working for myself because I'm a wrong/bad/loser sort of person is like deciding that the car won't start because it is a wrong/bad/loser sort of car—a popular way of looking at things, but popularity doesn't make it true. Life is a great deal more complex than people want to think it is. People want to believe that being, feeling, thinking, and doing what they are supposed to will get them everything they want. No problems, no hassles, no disappointments—do the right thing and get the right result. The flaw with this kind of thinking is simply that life is not that way.

We think because we can see how something "should" be ("should" being "could" with a personal bias), that if something is not that way, there is a mistake, something is wrong. It is the most obvious and completely unacceptable truth (to most people) that life has absolutely no interest in how we think it should be.

So, instead of focusing on what *should be* happening, let's focus on what *is* happening. I'm not working for myself. *How?* I don't know. I need to find out.

You notice that I didn't ask *why*, I asked *how*. Why?(!) Because it doesn't matter why. *Why* just takes us into our conditioned thinking patterns and away from the situation at hand. In the course of answering the question *how*, one will often answer the question *why*. But to answer the question *how* from answering *why* would be an utter fluke. "My car won't run." *Why?* We are returned immediately to the world of the three-year-old. "Why?" asks the child. "Because," answers the weary parent.

How takes us to interesting places. How is the ignition system functioning? Is it getting gas? Is there a spark? Will the engine turn over? *How* is movement. *How* reveals. *How* is *process*.

The following stories give us a glimpse into the importance of looking for the *how* that underlies a pattern of behavior.

THE MYSTERY OF THE MIDAS TOUCH

Ellen is a whiz at making money. She would be the first to tell you that she is not good at other aspects of life—relationships, health, and relaxation, to name a few—but she knows how to make money. People claim that she has the "Midas touch," in much the same way that certain gardeners are said to have a "green thumb."

At this point, one of Ellen's challenges is that people around her want her to work the magic for them. But she's found that she can't do that. She can only make money for herself, and only for a short time. After a certain point, she loses the money. One day everything just falls apart, as if she's jinxed, and she goes into a financial downward spiral.

When she's lost everything, or is close to it, she becomes deeply depressed, hearing hate-filled internal voices telling her that she deserves everything that's happening to her, and that she's a fake who deserves to be revealed for what she is. She becomes paralyzed, unable to leave her bed, obsessed with suicidal thoughts.

A few weeks later, she "wakes up." She has her old energy back, sees the possibilities in life, is eager to get back to the "real world," and turns her attention toward the thing that will make a lot of money.

❄   ❄   ❄

When the whole sequence of events was mapped out, and we got to the bottom of this pattern, I realized how similar Ellen's pattern was to that of another woman I worked with, although the content of their stories is completely different.

LOVE STORY

Bobbie had always struggled with depression, especially during her teen years and into her early 20s. In her 30s, she became involved with a man she absolutely worshiped. Rich was, in Bobbie's mind, the perfect human being. She had never been popular in school, being viewed as more of a brain than a beauty, so Rich was the football captain she had always secretly dreamed of.

To Rich, Bobbie was wonderful, brilliant, and attractive. He supported her fully, taking her side in every dispute with a boss, co-worker, or family member. Rich was strong and confident and always knew what Bobbie should do in any situation. All she had to do was tell him what was wrong, and he would tell her how to fix it. He wanted to be her whole world and was not happy sharing her—even with others who loved her.

It seemed like a match made in heaven—of course they would live happily ever after—but instead of being content with this situation, Bobbie felt herself slipping back into depression. This was, of course, extremely upsetting for her, not only because her past episodes left her with a dread of descending permanently into hopeless despair, but also because this was one situation that Rich couldn't deal with. He wanted to help, but he lost his enthusiasm when nothing he offered could fix her depression.

❄   ❄   ❄

As we worked on seeing *how* all this was happening, Bobbie made several painful yet illuminating discoveries. She realized how much Rich was like her mother. Her mother was loving and supportive—and controlling. Bobbie could never be angry with her mother, or disagree with her, because her mother was so wonderful. Instead, she learned to depress feelings about her mother. Naturally she was drawn to Rich; he was exactly like her earliest and most consistent experiences of love—supportive, good to her, and controlling. Eventually, she used the same weapon against his complete takeover of her life that she had learned with her mother—depressing the "negative" feelings and becoming someone he could not control. Rich was not interested in seeing through their conditioned patterns of relating, and instead, escalated the behaviors in an attempt to regain control of Bobbie and the relationship. She ended up leaving him.

In the ensuing years, Bobbie returned to the relationship twice. Both times, she realized later, she went back because she was growing and changing and felt out of control. Rich would quickly move into the role of providing boundaries and structure for her, only to have her move to the other side of the duality and begin to chafe under the externally imposed restrictions. She wanted to be free to be herself.

Bobbie eventually realized that she was using Rich to recreate a childhood survival pattern. Her mother had provided the structure in which she felt safe enough to explore her desires for freedom and autonomy. When her mother withdrew support, Bobbie would feel frightened and come back to the controlled environment. When she felt strong enough, through the support, she would feel angry at being controlled, go into a depression, come out of the depression with a desire to be free, and the whole thing would begin again. Despite her new understanding, Bobbie was amazed that each time she felt that life was too big, going too fast, *she had a nearly overwhelming urge to call Rich.*

The urge to repeat our childhood survival systems, which maintain our identity, is nearly irresistible; and egocentricity counts on us to revert to habits under stress. If Ellen made money and never lost it, what would happen to her identity as a depressed person? How would she be able to continue to believe she is a fake? Why should she become paralyzed and obsessed with suicidal thoughts? The cycle maintains itself: Ellen makes money and she is okay. But being a person who makes money is not who she *really* is, according to her conditioned identity—she is a fake who deserves to die. She loses the money, and now the truth is revealed—yes, she is indeed a fake. But that can last only so long—that reality loses its charge if there is nothing to compare it to. Hope returns, and Ellen starts the pattern over.

Similarly, Bobbie found herself drawn to the controlling hand of a partner as a way to perpetuate her childhood relationship with her mother. She would feel the desire to be free because she had the safety and security of a structured (controlling) relationship. But being free is not who she *really* is, according to her conditioned identity—she is a person who needs to be controlled in order to feel safe and secure. The very feeling of freedom triggers the conditioned desire to be controlled.

This full-circle nature of conditioning is one of the reasons we have such a hard time catching on to it—it doesn't seem to make sense. *I work and work to free myself of the things that have controlled my life so that my life can be bigger, better, fuller, more exciting, and the net result is that I feel frightened and dash back to the security of someone else controlling my life. I work hard to make money, and then being successful frightens me so much that I lose everything in order to once again feel like "myself."*

Conditioning is not just the side of the duality that we don't like; it is both ends of the continuum plus everything in between. We are not successful in seeing through what is keeping us stuck, because we focus only on what has been identified as the problem, which is not the problem. The problem (and it's not really a problem, it's simply a source of suffering) is the part of ourselves that survives by pointing a finger and saying *that* is the problem. The only problem that can actually be solved, the only problem that stands in the way of change, is the underlying conditioned belief system about who and how we need to be in order to survive. I may think that alcohol is my problem, but if I focus only on not drinking and pay no attention to the rest of my life, I will very likely continue to drink. If I decide to quit smoking but pay no attention to how smoking reinforces the survival structures of my life, I will very likely replace those cigarettes with food or fingernail-biting.

There may be those who wonder what the difference is between what we are discussing here and psychotherapy.

Depending on the therapist, the difference may be small, but awareness practice includes two factors that are not necessarily part of psychotherapy. First, in awareness practice, there is no assumption that something is wrong and needs to be fixed. Second, there is no outside authority; the only expert involved is the individual practicing self-awareness. With the guidance of someone who has experience in awareness practice, Ellen and Bobbie observe themselves and learn from what they see. The support they are offered is simply that of an encouraging, compassionate presence—a witness to their work.

In the next chapter, I will offer some specific ways to shift our awareness from content to process. We will also look at what stands in the way of our doing so.

CHAPTER THREE

AWARENESS:
To Sit Still and Notice

This is where I make my argument for meditation. In the way that I use the term, *meditation* is synonymous with *awareness practice,* and sitting meditation is one aspect of the whole process.

There are many types of meditation, which can be confusing. One can meditate to reduce stress, to take a time-out from life. One can meditate to focus the attention on a particular object to the exclusion of others. One can meditate to get a new perspective on a problem. One can meditate as a way of deepening a relationship with a supreme being.

My definition of *meditation* is "being present in conscious awareness." To be free of suffering, we must learn to be in the moment in which life is happening. In my experience, it takes a good deal of paying attention to the *attempts* to be in the moment to realize how *out* of the moment we are.

The second book I read on Zen gave instructions for a sitting meditation. I learned two things: (1) You sit in the full lotus position (the posture in which your legs are crossed, feet resting on thighs); and (2) you count your breaths from one to ten, then start over with one.

I began immediately. How I learned to sit is something I

explain to people when they are just beginning, because I think my experience may offer helpful information. From the time I read that description of a sitting meditation, I sat in the full lotus posture every moment I was not walking or lying down. I talked on the phone, read, had tea, and visited with friends while sitting in full lotus. When the pain became too much, I would release my legs, rest them, switch the one on top, and return to the position. By the time I left the monastery where I trained, I could sit in full lotus indefinitely, as long as I switched legs every couple of hours. The point I want to make is this: As difficult as it may seem, sitting in meditation position (full lotus or an alternative) is, with practice, quite possible. As with everything in life, it all depends on how much we want to do it. It comes down to willingness. (And it's helpful to know that an alternative to the full lotus includes sitting—with spine properly aligned—in a chair.)

The second step, counting the breaths, was a life-altering experience. The book suggested counting the breaths from one to ten, so that's exactly what I did. I counted breaths everywhere, all the time—in the shower, while I ate, as I worked, I counted breaths. It was hard to count breaths and carry on a conversation, although I learned to do this fairly well as long as the other person was talking and I was listening.

During that period of my life, I was driving back and forth between Oregon and the Bay Area of California with some regularity. I decided to count my breaths on a trip between San Jose and Medford. Ten hours of counting breaths!

I knew something was happening to me the first time I stopped for gas. Instead of my customary chip-on-the-shoulder attitude to people I encountered, I actually felt friendly toward them—for no reason! When I stopped for something to eat, it was as if I had been ingesting illegal substances: Everything was beautiful, colors were vibrant, people seemed so *dear*. By the time I reached my destination, I was ecstatic. My world seemed huge. Those things that I would have perceived as problems to solve just a day before, were now a joy. Nothing was a problem, nothing was wrong. I was in love with life; and everything was fun, interesting, exciting, and perfect.

I didn't know enough to recognize that for the first time, I was living in the moment. I didn't know that the reason I was so happy was that I had stepped free of the illusion of a separate self standing outside life and making judgments about each moment as a way to keep its place at the center of the universe. I just knew that counting breaths brought me to this new experience—and I wanted to count breaths from that moment on, for as long as I lived.

People ask me when they can stop counting breaths and go on to something more advanced. I just smile inside and hope that some day they do find an experience more advanced than counting breaths, because I know that then they will be blissful beyond telling. In the meantime, I encourage them to find out what counting has to offer before they move beyond it. The fact that they desire to go on to something else lets me know that they don't yet know what is available to them right here and now through this simple practice.

Practicing

So, let's begin here, now. Rest the book somewhere nearby so that it is easily retrievable but will not distract you. Turn your attention to your body as you take three long, full, relaxed breaths.

What did you notice?

Were you able to keep your attention on the breath?

What sensations were you aware of in your body?

Where were the sensations strongest?

Were you aware of any tension, discomfort, or pain?

Did your attention move around or stay focused on a particular point during the breaths?

What were your thoughts during the breaths?

Did you move your attention from the breath to the head or the eyes?

What emotions did you experience?

Where in your body did you experience these emotions?

How would you describe the emotions in language other than your thoughts about the emotion? (For example, when I feel sad, there is heaviness in my chest, like a 20-pound weight perched on top of my heart. My throat feels tight and full, as if something large is lodged in it, and my eyes are burning.)

Let's try it again. Set the book aside, and focus on your breath. Take three long, full breaths.

What were you aware of around you as you breathed?

What did you hear? What did you see? Smell?

Were you warm, cool, or just the right temperature?

Was there movement in your field of awareness? Were you aware of what was close to you? At a distance from you?

Did your thoughts wander?

Any questions? Comments? Memories? Fears? Irritation?

Let's try it again. Set the book aside and focus on your breathing. Take three more breaths.

What did you notice?

This is it: You are meditating.

Here is the biggest tip I can offer you: If you pay very close attention to exactly *how* you learn to pay attention, you will learn everything you need to learn. You will learn *how*; you will learn *process*. You will learn to learn.

Here are reports from three people doing the process of meditation outlined above:

FIRST-TIME MEDITATOR

I found myself dizzy and tired when I breathed deeply. I kept my attention on my breath and noticed tingling in my feet, tightness in my lungs, and restlessness and anxiety throughout. After the first three breaths, my attention moved around some, but returned to my breath, which began to feel like it was flowing more like water than air. I was aware of concerns and anxiety coming in and going out, as well as concerns as to whether or not anyone was watching me. I paid attention to my head at one point, while remaining attentive to my breath. The feelings I experienced were deep sadness, peace, tiredness, and warmth all over my body. These emotions manifested themselves physically as a heaviness and tightness in my chest and throat, and relaxation in my limbs. The third time, I was aware only of my breath and my thoughts—I didn't notice anything else around me. My thoughts wandered toward feelings of anxiety about not being sure how I'm supposed to be doing this.

EXPERIENCED MEDITATOR

When I took the first three breaths, I noticed that I think I'm making myself breathe. I noticed under that, a subtle but constant criticism for not breathing right. Lately, I've been acknowledging the fact that I'm not going to "get" meditation. The moment when I notice the breath is the only moment there is. The criticism comes afterward, through a voice that says things like, "Where have you been? You've been doing this for so long, and look how long it took you to get back to the breath." That's not meditation, it's self-hate.

I've realized I have this idea that there will be a time when the breath and being present becomes one long, continuous, blissful experience. So what is scary, and also liberating, is that—and this is true of my recent experiences—this moment is all there is. Noticing the breath as if for the first time, over and over again. That's what being present is—not having the past breath or a future breath to hold on to, or to create a continuous experience out of—it's like frame by frame. I'm alive, I'm breathing, here I am. Over and over again. It reminds me of dying and being born over and over again. It isn't what I thought being present would be like. I knew that I wouldn't be able to bring anything with me into death. Now I realize I can't bring anything with me even into the next moment.

DOUBTFUL MEDITATOR

I didn't notice much of anything. Most of the time, my mind just wandered, as it always does. Now and then, I'd remember to try to pay attention, and I'd notice how I felt or notice something that was going on, but instantly my mind would be off again. I'm not sure I can do this.

GRATEFUL MEDITATOR

Just wanted to report that yesterday I tried everything else to escape my negative feelings before I finally sat down and meditated for 35 minutes. Afterwards, I was less chained to my suffering, and went on with my day with a bit more freedom and gratitude. I feel a little more willing to sit today, which is a tremendous gift.

※　※　※

Please note: *Both new and experienced meditators can at times find themselves lost in doubt—or in gratitude.*

You will read, or people will tell you, that you must sit in the full lotus position for several hours each day if you are going to get anywhere as a meditator. You must clear your mind, change your life, and let go of your attachments if you are going to advance toward enlightenment. Now, I'm not going to tell you that those are utterly untrue statements, but I *will* tell you that the person who would take that advice doesn't need it. That person has already dropped enough attachments (or never had them) to have a mind that is much clearer than most. Here, we are talking to and about the rest of us.

As far as I can tell, that sort of information about meditation is the fastest way to be sure the rest of us will: (1) never meditate;

and (2) have one more thing to feel bad about. If, in fact, you sit down for five minutes a day, five days a week, and do the practice I just described, your life will quickly be all you wish it to be.

How can this be so? Aren't we back into knowing, getting, and doing? Remember this: Life is not reasonable, it is paradoxical.

When you stop trying to change, you will be different.

When you accept everything as it is, everything will have changed.

When you are no longer focused on knowing, you will know.

When you are no longer identified as a self, you will be self-confident rather than self- conscious.

When you are no longer interested in doing, you will be able to do anything.

When you do not care at all about success or failure, you will succeed.

Learning and Knowing

When practicing meditation, as I said when we tried it, we can *learn* to learn. And as we do that, we will also learn that there is nothing to know.

Generally, though, as socially engineered creatures, we are not interested in learning; we want to *know*. Knowing is critical in the conditioned scheme of things because it means survival. Knowing means acceptance, approval, doing the right thing, and being the right person. If you know, you will be right. If you are right, you are good. If you are good, you will be loved. If you are loved, you will survive. And knowing keeps us from being fully present.

Learning, on the other hand, is merely a necessary but often difficult, uncomfortable, and dreaded stage along the way to knowing. Can you remember the last time you really enjoyed learning? Not learning *something*, but the actual business of learning—which, let's face it, starts with not knowing.

I have a friend who's a skater. If I asked her, she might say she loves to learn new things in skating. Looking more closely, however, we might discover that what she loves is to learn new *things*—new steps, new jumps, and new combinations of moves. That is, the process of learning is enjoyable only when it leads quickly and smoothly to knowing something new. How long would she enjoy the learning if she never got to *know* something, if she never acquired a new skill?

Here's another element. When we learn something, we expect to be successful. If I am going to learn to make furniture, I want, after a reasonable amount of time, to be able to make something good. "Good"—what a trap. Were you one of those people who found out you weren't good at art? Remember when all you needed was some paper and a box of crayons? Do you remember finding out it was important to stay inside the lines? How about sports? Remember when all the fun you needed was just to go play? Then play got organized into patterns (games), and you had to perform a certain way (well), and suddenly you were either good or bad depending on how well you met the standards of that game. Were you ever the last person chosen for a team? Do you remember how humiliating that felt? The point is that if we impose such standards on ourselves, if we require "success" for our efforts, we are likely to avoid learning. When we avoid learning, we needlessly restrict our lives.

I really enjoyed the first half hour or so that I played golf. I had been attracted to golf from the first moment I saw it, but as a poor kid in a small town, I had no chance to play. In middle age,

I met a woman (the editor, illustrator, and designer of most of the books I write) who was a golf pro, and she agreed to teach me to play. I was overjoyed and went into the learning process with great excitement: holding my body and the club in that strange posture, swinging the club, trying to hit the little ball, the thrill of making contact and seeing the ball move. . . . But as my standards grew higher, the thrill diminished proportionally. I began to want to hit the ball straight, to get it into the air, to make it go farther. Each swing, each contact, each hit, became an opportunity for disappointment. Golf went from pure joy to the deadly earnest contest it is for many golfers. The pleasure did not return until I quit keeping score. Only then could I focus on the process of the game and actually enjoy *playing*.

Learning is very different from knowing. Learning involves change, movement, and the unknown. Learning is *current* (meaning now, but the association with *flow* is also significant). In the learning process, we are vulnerable. Learning can be dangerous. Learning is alive. Learning is life.

The Illusion of Control

If I'm going to invest my time in learning something, I want to be able to do it well in a reasonable amount of time. For most of us a "reasonable amount of time" means "immediately." We think we should already know—everything! Almost all the people I work with—intelligent, aware, bright, educated people— still believe at a very deep level that they should already know what they could not possibly know: what is going to happen next.

The illusion of control is based on three assumptions: (1) We *need* control (life is not something we can trust); (2) we *should* control; and (3) we *can* control. When life is defined as dangerous and the only way to guarantee survival is to know—even knowing what you cannot know—there is no room for learning.

In such a world, knowing is all that matters. Knowing is control, making sure everything proceeds as one wishes.

The expectation and the belief that we should know what we do not know sustains our illusion of having control in our lives. If we can step outside that illusion, it becomes apparent that we are simply in this place and in this moment, with no knowledge of what's going to happen in the next moment, so we have no alternative to accepting everything exactly as it is.

Yet, because of our conditioning, we are blindly addicted to the illusion of control. Let's say that you put the last of your savings in a sure thing on the stock market, and the company goes belly-up. You tell yourself, "I should have known better!" You meet the perfect person and fall madly in love, only to discover that the person lies to you. "I should have known better!" You take a fabulous job, and then find out that you were just hired to fill in until the CEO's girlfriend gets out of college. "I should have known better!" If any of these situations had worked out as hoped, you would see yourself as brilliant, on top of things, and doing it right. But because they did not go the way you wished, you feel that you have failed to control life, which means that you've done something wrong and are being punished.

In fact, no one knows what the future will bring. We can make educated guesses. We can play the odds. But we cannot *know*. There is no control. And, contrary to what we experienced in childhood, not getting what you want is not a punishment.

MARTIN

When I considered what issue I would like to practice awareness with, I came up with this: my need/tendency/ desire to be in control/be right. The part of me that has this need would state it this way: "I want to know everything that is going on. I want to decide what should be done and how. And I want everyone to do it my way."

Feedback from other people, as well as my own efforts to pay attention, suggest that this issue is not new. Yet I made a discovery in answering the question: "How long has this been an issue in your life?" A voice in me answered, "Issue? What issue? There is no problem here. This is exactly how I want life to be. I have no problem with being in control." When I am identified with the controlling self, as I often am, there is no problem, no issue, nothing to be changed. When I am less identified with it, I can see the suffering it causes me and others.

I am curious about this part of me that believes that everything must be in control. Who is he? What does he want? How does he see the world? What threatens him? What sets him off? What can he teach me? I can see that he is not the most wonderful person to be around, yet I don't want to push him away. I want to be his friend and see how I might assist him.

This feels very helpful already—to see that some part of me didn't see the issue as an issue, and that some other part of me doesn't see that part as a problem to be solved.

PAT

The problem I'd like to examine is my feeling that I need to control life. I can remember as far back as my early teens feeling that life was messy, ugly, and out of control. I thought people were lazy, myself especially, and I vowed to fight that. I'd write in my journals and make rigid plans for myself and keep them for a while, but then I'd be unable to keep such tight control, and I would become filled with despair and self-hatred.

In some form or another, I've been fighting that battle ever since. I continue to make plans for myself, and even when I can recognize that my need to control everything is part of the problem, I still approach it by trying to fig- ure out how to control my need to control.

My focus on control sucks the joy right out of my life in so many situations. Instead of seeing the cup half (or more) full, I see it as about to tip over and spill and make a horrible mess. I'm constantly anticipating the worst, filling my mind with everything that might go wrong, and telling myself that in doing so, I'm keeping it from going wrong. In fact, I'm just guaranteeing that I will be mis- erable.

I fill my mind with "if onlys": if only I had more free time, more money, fewer responsibilities, then I'd be able to get enough control of my life so that everything would work. Indeed, as I write this, I realize how much I still believe at some deep level that I really can have every- thing under control (whatever that means), and I just need to keep trying harder to arrange my external cir- cumstances in such a way that it will happen. Perhaps I'm a bit more subtle about it than I used to be. Now I can tell myself that dedicating myself to a spiritual practice will help me get everything under control. (In that way, my desire for control is actually a good thing, because it motivates me to pursue something that is really good.)

If I can't control something, I start disowning it. Work is mostly out of my control, so I don't really care about work. I just go there because I have to. The weeds in the yard seem out of control, so I stop caring about them. They're just things that get in the way of me having the freedom to get everything truly under control and doing exactly the right thing.

I can never meet my standard of having things under

control, at least for any length of time. Yet I continue to believe that it is absolutely critical that I get things under control. So I constantly see myself as failing, and I hate myself for it. I am in a state of mild panic much of the time, because I'm afraid of what will happen as a result of my not having things under control. And I get depressed a lot, because I never seem to be able to achieve the control I'm aiming for. I start thinking, What's the use?

❋   ❋   ❋

Are these two people benefiting from their belief that control is possible, desirable, and necessary?

The illusion of control is the largest element in the program of social conditioning designed to keep the individual in line. We are not only supposed to know what cannot be known—the future—we are also supposed to be able to control everything. So from the beginning, we set out to accomplish the impossible. When control proves impossible, the response we're likely to hear is, "What? You don't have control of your life? What's the matter with you? Try harder!" No wonder we're afraid of the very thought of not having control.

We can use being afraid to our advantage, if we pay attention to it. A piece of information we can always count on to help us in our practice of awareness is this: Fear is always egocentricity. Period. Since awareness practice aims to unveil every illusion that stands between our conditioned ideas about ourselves and our true nature, fear is the thing to follow. *What we experience as fear is the feeling that egocentricity sends out when it's threatened, when awareness is getting too close.*

Our conditioning makes us too afraid to go back and question the original premise to which we devote ourselves: that we must control life. As we practice awareness, though, we see through the elaborate schemes of conditioning by which our lives are run, and we build the courage to face the fear that controls us. We realize that we are controlled by the fear of a loss of control.

People are conditioned to not want to hear "I don't know" from authority figures. Rather than frighten the patient, the medical doctor will say something such as, "It's nothing to worry about," when "I don't know" would be the truth. Perhaps concern would be an appropriate response for the person if the expert doesn't have an answer. Instead, the patient is patted on the head and told not to worry.

What would our lives be like if we realized that controlling life is not possible?

THE KIND CONTROLLER

Ron and Penny have been married for 25 years. They have been through some rough patches, and both would say that their union is solid. Ron "wears the pants" in the family. He makes the big decisions but is not authoritarian—they discuss things before he decides. This arrangement has always worked well for them. Ron is a good provider, a good father, and takes his responsibilities seriously.

In fact, Ron takes his responsibilities so seriously that if he is thwarted in his efforts to do what must be done, he can become quite angry, and on occasion, verbally abusive. Ron has a number of behaviors, ranging from silent withdrawal to threats of punishment, that he uses to make sure his family is safe and secure. The first time I suggested "verbal abuse" to Ron, he was stunned. He was also hurt and resentful. How could I accuse him of such a thing when all he's ever done is take care of his family?

Ron is firmly in the grasp of the illusion of control. He believes, without being aware that he believes it, that if everyone will just do and be what he dictates, everyone will be safe and happy. When someone goes against his program, he sees that person as the enemy, a threat to his (and therefore everyone's) well-being. He then feels as if he's on his own in a hostile world, and, operating from the illusion of separation, he attacks.

The person calling the shots is not the only one operating out of an illusion of control. Penny has her own illusory world in place. The way she controls her world is through: (1) manipulating Ron, and (2) blaming him for her life. Of course, they're both playing the same game, because Ron certainly manipulates Penny and blames her for the parts of his life that don't work. We can all recognize this in ourselves. It is expressed in terms such as "If only . . ." and "If it weren't for . . ." When we're under the spell of one of these illusions, we tend to blame—ourselves or others.

"I'm just trying to make things work," Ron says. "You're not helping, you know. If you would just [fill in the blank], it would be a lot easier." Then, when feeling defeated by his lack of ability to make life the way it should be, Ron slides over to the other side of the duality and blames himself: "I know it's my own fault. I'm just a loser. I can never get anything to work—never have, never will. I don't know why I don't just give up."

Ron could notice that this internal dialogue has two prominent features: (1) I'm in control. I know what's going on, what would be successful, how things are and should be, why it's not working, and who's fault it is; and (2) I'm surviving. I'm not going to give up! It's me against them—even when *them* is *me*!—and I have no intention of letting go of this drama that puts me squarely center stage, the star in the theater of life.

Now, in case this is not completely obvious to everybody, let me spell it out. The survival system requires being right and being in control even when "being right and in control" is the result of being wrong and out of control. (Ah, the paradox of Zen!) *"If all of you will listen to me and do as I say, we'll be fine."* (Meaning, I'm right and in control; I know what is happening and how it will turn out.) Pressure and stress build, my demands increase, the standards are raised. Finally, it becomes clear (although never acknowledged) that my way is not working. I blame all of you. *"Why won't you listen to me? If you had done as I 'asked,' we wouldn't be in this situation."* (I'm right and in control; I know what is happening and how it will turn out—even though we're now on the opposite end of the duality.) Things continue to go downhill. The situation is hopeless. I shift to a different part of my conditioning. *"Why do I keep trying? I can't make this work. It's all my fault. I should have known better."* (I'm still right and in control; I know what is happening and how it will turn out.) I give up. Time passes. I regain my strength—and move back to the other end of the continuum. *"If all of you will listen to me and do as I say, we'll be fine."* I was mistaken before; it can work, because I know what to do—I am right and in control.

As they used to say in those ABC-TV sports promos: It's "the thrill of victory, the agony of defeat." I may be trying to make you think that this is horrible and I hate the whole thing, but I wouldn't change for the world. Why? Because with egocentricity, with our attachment not to our present survival but to the childhood survival system created by our conditioning, while there is the thrill of victory and the agony of defeat, there is also an equal agony of victory and thrill of defeat.

Ron and Penny remain committed to their lives together, and now they are also committed to finding out what the real payoff has been for being together in the way they always have. As they see more clearly that their conditioned way of being is not getting them what they truly *want,* but rather what they *don't* want, they are each willing to make an honest assessment of how they are contributing to their unsuccessful dynamic. For the first time, through working on this process together, their differences are bringing them closer together rather than farther apart.

Personal Survey on Control

- What is control?

- Can you recall a time when you had a positive experience of being "in control"? A negative experience of being "in control"? A negative experience of being "out of control"? A positive experience of being "out of control"?

- Where do you feel "control" in your body?

- How do you maintain the illusion of control?

- What do you trade for the illusion of control?

- What beliefs are supported by the illusion of control?

Remember: *You are looking for awareness in order to better see the ways in which you have been conditioned. Your conditioning is not the same as who you truly are. Please do not allow conditioning to use your awareness against you.*

Nowhere to Go

In meditation—in learning to be present in the moment we are in—we are not trying to *get anywhere*. We are not participating in a process of *learning*, so much as a process of *unlearning*. We are returning to our original state of being. When we arrived on this earth, we were not "someone who is present"; we were simply *presence*.

A moment of unconsciousness is a moment of life you don't have. A moment of conscious awareness is a moment of living—and life, when we are present to it, is always good, regardless of the content.

But how can sitting five minutes a day, five days a week, make a difference? How can sitting for five minutes, five days a week, allow me to move from a conditioned, programmed, out-of-the-moment, robotic (do we sense a bias here?) approach to life to one of conscious, present, attentive focus?

Initially, it is not the sitting that makes the difference; it is spending a period of time in an internal atmosphere of acceptance. When we sit for five minutes a day in this kind, open, interested way, we soon want to sit for ten minutes. Remember, it's not *what*, it's *how*. When you approach your life with the attitude that there is something wrong with you, that something needs to be done to fix yourself, life is not much fun. Nobody likes to be told they're wrong and need to be corrected. It is not uplifting. It is destructive.

Perhaps this is a good time to confess that the title of this book is something of a trick. We are conditioned from day one to believe that there is somewhere to go and something to get. We have to get from here to there. *I need to stop being the way I am, so I can be the way I should be, so I can get to where I need to go to get the things I want.* No—not true, not any of it. In fact, exactly the opposite is true:

> *Any moment other than this one does not exist. As long as we look to the future, we will live in dissatisfaction.*
>
> *We give up everything that is possible for us, everything we could ever want, which is all that is, in this moment,*

*in order to chase an illusion that will never lead
anywhere except to suffering.*

There is not and never was anything wrong with us.

*We have been sold, and we have bought, a completely
false picture of life.*

*Rather than going from where we are to where we want
to be, we need to remember to be where we are, here,
now. We don't need to go anywhere else or do anything
else. We don't need to go from here to there; we need to
return from there to here.*

To take our first step toward awareness, we need to know
where we are now. To discover this, we must let go of the idea
that we *know*. To see where we are now, it is necessary to be vulnerable, present, in this moment, open—and *not* knowing.

Why is not knowing necessary? Because we cannot simultaneously hold on to what we know, dragging dead information
around, and be available to what is present in this moment. I cannot simultaneously attend to my impression of you during our
last meeting and be present to who you are in this meeting. I cannot swing a baseball bat the way I always have while simultaneously swinging it in a new way. The old has to go in order to
make room for the new.

Now, it is true that I may decide that the old way of swinging
that bat is preferable. But I cannot actually *learn* that until I am
willing to experience both ways with fresh, uncluttered, unconditioned perception.

The first step is to face clearly how I am in this moment,
accept it, and release myself from the grip of conditioning that
keeps me that way. Only then can I make conscious choices to be
other than the way I've been conditioned to be.

We are taught to feel insecure when we know that we don't know. But it is only ego that is insecure when we realize we don't know. Consciously choosing to know that you do not know is liberation. "You must become as little children" is profound spiritual advice. Little children do not know. They do not know that knowing is an option. They are simply present to their experience, living whatever life is in that moment.

Many people recoil in horror from the notion that we should become like that. "But little children can't protect themselves!" That is true—*and neither can we!* Neither group has any guarantees, but the difference is that one group doesn't have a problem with that and just lives, while the other group is made miserable by the fact that they cannot have what was never a choice.

Seeing into the Issue by Shifting Our Focus

The next question to ask about the issue you are working on is this:

What stops me from [working for myself]?

Like the title of this book, this is a slightly tricky question. Asking "What stops me?" has me looking for some obstacle in the belief that once it is eliminated, I can do what I want. The real question is, "How am I stopped from working for myself?"

The phrasing is important, because we easily slip into re-forming the question to be, "How do I stop myself?" That is *not* a good question, because it can carry the implication that I know full well what I'm doing, and I continue to do it out of some form of cussedness. With the not-working-for-myself issue, I know that's not so because I don't have a clue about what is going on, never mind who's to blame! I want to do this thing, and I am not able to, even though I possess the necessary qualities to accomplish what I want. It's not that I lack the skills or the time or the interest, it's just that somehow it never happens. Or, it hasn't happened yet. But I am going to find out *how* it doesn't happen. How do I find that out? I watch. I pay very close attention from the moment I decide (once again) that I am going to work for myself until the moment I realize I am *not* working for myself.

The most difficult aspect of this paying attention part of the program is that to be successful, one must very nearly lose interest in whether or not one accomplishes one's goal. For a good while now, I have been trying to arrange my life so I can work for myself. I try, I fail. I try, I fail. I feel frustrated, frightened, and hopeless, but I'm not even focused on how I feel. I am focused on trying and failing.

A more specific question to ask:

What do I do instead of [working for myself]?

I have a friend who says that she can never get a project done because before she can do anything, she has to clean her desk, and by the time she cleans her desk, she's tired and has lost interest in the project she was going to do. She ends up with a very clean desk and a lot of suffering over her inability to complete a project.

People who are chronically late often have no idea how that happens to them. They have the best intentions, feel really bad about their tardiness, resent other people's demands, but just can't stop being late. When they start to focus on *how* they're late, they will begin to see that they have a whole host of activities that they perform between the time they would need to leave in order to be on time and the actual time they leave.

It can be helpful to take notes. My friend might say, "If I take notes, I'll never get around to my projects!" The chronically late person would no doubt be convinced that taking notes would guarantee terminal tardiness. That reaction is part of a scam being run by the conditioning that is in place to keep each of us as we are. It's not laziness or stupidity or inadequacy that keeps us from accomplishing the things we know we want to accomplish—it's a conditioned pattern.

Being different—which for the people just described would mean completing a project and being on time, respectively—requires change. Change is threatening to an established identity. Our conditioning is a survival system put into place long ago to ensure that change does not happen and the identity remains intact. We can test this theory simply by attempting to do something different, whether it's "positive" or "negative." When we attempt change, our conditioned identity is threatened and tends to contract, trying to close down as a way of fending off this new danger. We can see that kind of contraction in cases when people faced with death cannot or will not stop smoking or stop drinking alcohol or change their diet.

We are conditioned to believe that we do the things we do because we want to, that we are choosing what we do. We are conditioned to believe that we do what we do for our own benefit. When push comes to shove, we have an opportunity to see that the survival of our identity as a separate self is based on control, maintenance, routine, and sameness and will not be altered.

So, a helpful check-in when you hear yourself protest that if you do something different you will *never* accomplish whatever it is you want to do is to remind yourself that you are currently *not* accomplishing what you want, and that attempting a new solution to your problem cannot make the situation worse.

Here are some questions to consider:

- Have you ever resolved a problem that seemed unresolvable?

- If you cannot resolve this issue, should you be killed?

- How long will you be dead before this issue ceases to be a problem?

Now, I am going to turn my attention *away* from this trying and failing, and *toward* the process I go through, the steps I take *not* to work for myself. The next chapter is about the importance of bringing in a helpful attitude: compassion for myself.

CHAPTER FOUR

COMPASSION:
Befriending Yourself

If I were to sit down next to you and say, in a harsh, critical tone of voice, "What is the matter with you, anyway?" how open do you think you would be to sharing your deepest thoughts and feelings with me? How vulnerable would you be willing to be? Do you suppose you might feel a little defensive? Might you feel safer just responding with what you believe will be the "right answer" rather than considering what's really happening and possibly exploring deeper places within yourself?

Please consider how often a child is approached by an adult with a "What's-the-matter-with-you" attitude. No wonder we learn to hide our real selves. In such a situation, being unavailable is an intelligent survival strategy.

Now, suppose I sat down next to you and asked in a kind, respectful, caring, interested way, "How are you doing?" and when you respond, I listen and nod and offer encouragement. No judgments, no agenda, no ideas about how you should be—just accepting you as you are and being interested in how that is. Do you think you would be more open to me, more willing to let me see who you are and what you're like?

The Secret Ingredient

This brings us to what is, for me, the secret ingredient in the process we are learning. (It's not secret in the sense that no one knows about it—almost everyone knows it exists.) Once again, it's not *what*, it's *how*. This ingredient is secret only in the way that mustard might be a secret ingredient that turned an ordinary dish into an extraordinary one. "Who would have thought mustard could do that?"—secret in that sense. We all know that mustard exists, but it would never occur to us that using mustard in that way would make such a huge difference.

In the awareness practice we are talking about here—and in our lives—the secret ingredient is *compassion*. We all know (or think we know) that compassion exists and what it is, but almost no one knows how to use it. Just as a spice will take a dish from ordinary to extraordinary, compassion will take a life from ordinary to extraordinary.

There is one huge and happy breakdown in this analogy. If you use too much of a seasoning, you can ruin a dish. It takes an expert to find that fine line between not enough and too much. But compassion cannot be overused—the more, the better!

It is very important, I must hasten to add, that we learn what compassion actually is. Again, if you pay close attention to *how you learn* what compassion is, you will learn *how to learn* what *anything* is. If you assume you already know what compassion is—that is, if you allow your conditioned mind to dictate your relationship with compassion, you will never truly experience compassion. What you believe is compassion will be nothing more than an assumption.

An example: "The Buddha saw their suffering and his heart was filled with compassion." What does that mean? "Well," says our conditioned mind, "I guess it means that the Buddha felt sorry for them. He could see from his highly evolved perspective that they were lost in greed, hatred, and delusion. I suppose that's why he was kind to them instead of being hard on them, because he knew they were suffering. I wonder if that means he was suffering. If he felt sad for them, he must have been suffering. I know when I feel sad, I'm suffering. I guess what we're doing is *trying* to end suffering rather than actually being able to end suffering."

Can you see in that thought process something we can each relate to? The conditioned mind just leapfrogs along, making connections, adding a bit here and a bit there, until suddenly something it has no idea about is something it *knows*. Later, someone asks that student of Buddhism about ending suffering and gets a confident assurance that "the Buddha taught that suffering cannot actually be ended, but we need to work at it anyway," and neither person is aware that the information being passed along has no basis in truth.

If we were paying attention in the learning-rather-than-knowing way, we would question our assumption that we know anything about anything. Especially, we could be suspicious of our assumption that we can know what someone like the Buddha meant. When we hear that Jesus said, "Love one another as I have loved you," one part of us may be silently screaming, "But—*how?*" while another part is certain that it knows who loves correctly and who doesn't, what correct love looks like, when it's happening and what should be done about it when it's not, and on and on and on.

What I am suggesting here is a healthy dose of humility. Please take note: Humility is not self-hate. Humility is modest and unpretentious, yes; it's not arrogant or proud. But being modest and unpretentious does not mean that there's something wrong with you. Not assuming that we know everything does not mean we are stupid. Knowing that we do not know is the beginning of wisdom.

In awareness practice, we cultivate a fresh, open, receptive perception—like that of a child. When Jesus said, "You must become as little children," I think what he meant is this: We must be willing to set aside the knowing, smart, clever, sophisticated mind of the socially conditioned person to return to the innocent, authentic, "new" mind of our original being.

Experiencing Compassion

In the "back to the land" movement of the 1970s, I moved to the outback of Oregon to grow my own vegetables and build a cabin. I began by digging out the side of a hill for the foundation. Oregonians will tell you that their state has two seasons—dust and mud. I can promise you that those substances thinly conceal some of the rockiest terrain a person could ever try to dig in.

Toward the end of the summer, a neighbor, Ralph, strolled down the pair of ruts that served as a road to my pit-on-its-way-to-becoming-a-cabin.

"Gosh, I wish I'd known you were doing this," he drawled, pushing his cap back and scratching his head. "I build roads. I coulda brought the backhoe down here and dug this out in a coupla hours."

I consoled myself with the thought that having a huge, smelly, noisy piece of equipment rip up the earth would have been cheating on the do-it-yourself simplicity of the "back to the land" ethic.

Ralph was canvassing the area for someone who could help him with a pet problem—actually, a problem pet, as it turned out. His neighbors had gone on vacation and left their three dogs with him, but he had been called away unexpectedly and was looking for volunteers to take on his dog-sitting responsibilities. He had found someone to take in the two big dogs, who were fine outside, but not the "yappy little lap dog."

I had grown up with a German shepherd and never thought any other type of dog worthy of consideration, certainly not a "yappy little lap dog." But, wanting to be seen as a good neighbor (especially by a guy with a backhoe), I said, sure, I'd take the little dog while Ralph was away.

I had seen the dog as she chased my car and tagged along behind bigger, longer-legged animals as they traveled around the neighborhood. I remembered her particularly because I had strong opinions about people who don't take care of their pets. That little dog was scruffy and dirty, her matted hair sticking out in clumps all over her body. And, at about a foot tall, she didn't seem to be a good candidate for a long career as a car-chaser.

When Ralph delivered the goods the next day, he told me the dog's name was Tuffy. "And by the way," Ralph said, "the owners ended up with Tuffy when somebody died, and they really don't want her, so if you could find a good home for her. . . ."

I don't know when I realized I was in love. I don't think it was during the holding-her-down- and-bathing-and-clipping-her phase of our new relationship. It may have been when I took her on one of my regular rambles through the woods. I remember watching her run so fast down a hill that she lost control of her short little legs and rolled head over heels to the bottom. Then she got up, shook herself, and came tearing after me. In that moment, I knew her name was not Tuffy, but Toughie, and I sensed that she had found that good home she needed.

Over the years, people have confessed to me, in an embarrassed, self-conscious tone, that the "person" they care for most is an animal. "Oh," I assure them, "I know exactly what you mean. The love of my life was a dog." An animal provided my first experience of unconditional love. An animal taught me the meaning of compassion.

Defining Compassion

The word *compassion* is often used in the same sense as sympathy or pity. For example, we say we feel compassion for those less fortunate than ourselves; we feel compassion toward those who are struggling or ill or grieving. I think this merging of compassion with sympathy or pity is unfortunate. I would like us to look in a different direction.

Compassion doesn't mean feeling sorry for another. Literally, it means "to suffer with." To me, compassion is an experience of respect, of admiration, of appreciation. When someone is going through a difficult or painful time and we admire their courage, respect their journey, and offer support—that is compassion. Compassion doesn't assume there's something wrong that needs to be fixed or changed. Compassion is a step beyond sympathy in that, while we might feel sad that someone is having a difficult time, we do not assume that anything should be different. We cannot know if relieving someone's difficult circumstances would be the best thing for them or not—as suggested by the story of the monkey who grabs a fish out of the water and takes it to the top of a tree to save it from drowning.

Compassion is *identity with.* It brings us together in the sense of nonseparation. We feel oneness; nothing happens to you that doesn't happen to me. We take heart and are supported in that unity.

When you have compassion, you put yourself in position to be transformed by life. Many people have the experience of hearing about a tragedy and feeling sympathy, but thinking, *Thank God that's not me.* We feel sympathy, but there is separation. Sympathy will break your heart; compassion will break your heart open.

What is happening when we feel for or with another when we are moved in that way? I would suggest that for a brief moment, at a level most of us are unaware of, there is an experience that the "other" is not other. For just a flash, in a timeless, spaceless nonplace, we are one; we are not separate. A child falls down, a friend is disappointed, and we intuitively sense their goodness, their innocence, and their inherent purity. We feel that same goodness; we *are* that goodness. Our heart opens to that other being. That is compassion.

If you are willing to consider this as a possibility, you will see why sitting still and paying close attention at the most subtle levels is essential to this work. This type of insight—this nonseparation—tends not to be available to us as we are racing around through life, busy with and distracted by a myriad of "whats."

Uncovering Compassion

Can we learn to return to that childlike, innocent acceptance? Can we live from that awareness? Can we see ourselves in and *from* that nonseparate reality? Can we see that we are good and dear and trying so very hard? Can we feel *for* ourselves? Can we feel *with* ourselves?

Yes, we can, but we must first see exactly how we have learned not to feel compassion for ourselves, how we manage to withhold compassion from ourselves. We must learn how to let go of the conditioning that keeps us from having compassion for ourselves.

Is this selfish? Is this self-indulgent? No, for this reason: *It is not possible to feel for someone else what we do not feel for ourselves.* If you don't have compassion for yourself, you won't have compassion for anyone else. You will perhaps spend a good deal of your time and energy hating yourself for not being compassionate, but that won't make you compassionate.

I challenge anyone to find a single individual of recognized spiritual attainment who would say that you must hate yourself in order to have compassion for others. (Would *anybody* say that? Actually, we are told that all the time by our conditioning.) Jesus said, "As you do unto the least of my brethren, so you do unto me." As you treat yourself, you are treating Jesus. Sobering thought.

We must learn to recognize what is ego and what is authenticity, absolutely. We must learn to live from our hearts and not our egocentric conditioning, no doubt. That is what we are doing here. And the first step is to find compassion for ourselves within ourselves.

More Practice

In sitting meditation, we have the perfect opportunity to practice compassion toward ourselves. And since there is no end to our need to find compassion for ourselves, let us once again enter into the experience of meditation.

*Breathing in and breathing out. Noticing everything.
Allowing everything to be exactly as is. Relaxed, comfortable, not exerting or trying. Not holding onto anything,
not resisting or pushing anything away. Everything is just
as it is. Breathing.*

*The breath comes in, the body expands. The breath goes
out, the body contracts. Awareness rests deep in the belly
and expands outward. No boundaries, nothing left out. The
attention rests in the awareness. Breathing in. Breathing
out. Present. Here. Right here. In this moment.*

*Inhaling. Exhaling. Nowhere to go. Nothing to do.
Just noticing.*

*The mind wanders. Just notice, see where it goes. Ah, that.
Ah, going there, yes. No problems, not a difficulty.*

*Now, let's come back here. Attention returns to awareness.
Patient, compassionate, kind, gentle. Nothing wrong.*

Here we are, breathing. Sensations arise and pass away. Breathing. Thoughts arise and pass away. Just breathing. Emotions arise and pass away. Still breathing.

Lists of things to do arise, along, perhaps, with a sense of urgency, and as we breathe, peacefully, calmly, they pass away. In this moment, open to all that is, accepting, allowing, breathing.

In the beginning, just learning to sit for a few moments with this attitude is an enormous task. But if we can approach ourselves with compassion, the task will be easy and enjoyable. As Krishnamurti has said, "What is important in meditation is the quality in the mind and the heart. It is not what you achieve, or what you say you attain, but the quality of the mind that is innocent and vulnerable."

How Conditioning Blocks Compassion

When we find that sitting in meditation is anything but easy and enjoyable, it can be helpful to look for what we are doing instead of just sitting there and paying attention. Very often, we will find that we are caught up in finding fault with ourselves, others, and everything around us. Let's examine two forms of that.

Judgment

A fascinating wrinkle in the insane world of conditioning is that it is considered wrong to judge. Judging, we are taught, makes us bad. We should not be critical of others. Meanwhile, our lives are focused on the comparisons and subsequent judgments that arise from our ability to remember and discriminate—

the very ability that makes social conditioning possible. A child grows up knowing he wants to do well in school, get good grades, and have the approval of his teachers. He is encouraged to notice how well he is doing in comparison to everyone else and to beat them to the punch at every possible opportunity. He is supposed to do this while never having an unfavorable opinion about the people he is focused on defeating. Another child knows she is supposed to be prettier, smarter, and more popular than all the other girls without ever having a negative judgment about any of them.

Yet, according to conditioning, it is not only acceptable but essential to judge oneself. Judgment of oneself and the punishment that follows is the way we ensure good behavior. And, of course, it is always acceptable for groups of people, ostensibly serving the greater good of all, to get together to judge and punish those who do not behave according to the standards of the group—from criminals to nations who persist in following their own standards.

I find awareness of judgment to be an extraordinarily helpful tool in revealing egocentric social conditioning. I can learn a lot about myself by watching how I judge others. I can see my social conditioning in every thought and word about "them." I encourage people to judge freely. Judge, admit your judgments to yourself, use your judgments for self-awareness, and don't believe that they have anything to say about anyone or anything except your own conditioning.

Self-Improvement

The second form of finding fault is trying to change yourself. Self-improvement is social conditioning's secret weapon. As long as you're trying to be anyone's idea (including your conditioned self's idea) of how you should be, you are bound to stay the same.

It is a law of nature. If you think you've changed, look to see if that's true, and if it is, look to see how that happened.

Dieting is a good example of the socially conditioned trying-to-change, self-improvement loop in which nothing does change. Let's say I'm overweight. What does my social conditioning offer me on this subject? "You shouldn't be overweight," or even "You are overweight because you are an undisciplined, indulgent, greedy pig." The same is conveyed by constantly checking my appearance in mirrors and noticing the bulge here or the roll there or by checking how other people look and comparing my appearance with theirs.

In the situation of being overweight, my conditioning tells me what to do: *Go on a diet.* The kind of diet I select is conditioned, and how I approach it is conditioned.

As I begin the diet on one side of the duality, guess what is happening on the opposite side? That's right—"not dieting" is revving up. I forge ahead, I lose some weight, and just as I'm starting to feel good, a campaign of sabotage is launched from the other end. After a time, my identity shifts from being the person who is losing weight to being the person who wants to eat what I want to eat. End of diet. Preservation of conditioned identity. Yep, I'm just an undisciplined, indulgent, greedy pig.

Let's take an example from the financial realm. I look around and notice that other people have more money than I have. They're driving better cars, living in bigger houses in better neighborhoods, sending their kids to better schools, and having more exotic vacations. What's wrong with me? Conditioning has the answer: "You're a loser. That's why they're all better off than you are. You're a loser. Always have been, always will be." (Helpful, isn't it?)

In such circumstances, I turn to my conditioned mind to tell me what to do. What it tells me—what I should do and how I should do it—is programmed. Subliminally, I get conditioned messages about who I will be when I follow this program and how I will feel: no longer stupid, but smart. I'm going to get another job, or a part-time job, go back to school, stop watching TV, learn about investing—yes! I am moving ahead. So is the other side of the duality, circling around to close the loop. Soon I'm tired. I don't want to do all this stuff. I want to relax. Life is too short . . . where is that remote control? The conditioned mind breathes a sigh of relief. Not only am I back where I belong, but I will stay where I belong because I have just received irrefutable proof that I am, in fact, a stupid loser.

So, for those of you who believe you have changed, is it because you are currently on the other end of some continuum? Or have you seen through the illusion created by your conditioning and stepped off the continuum altogether?

Here is the point I wish to make on this subject: Stepping off the continuum is not a form of self-improvement. Stepping off the continuum is not the result of a program of change. Stepping off the continuum is a natural result of awareness. Real change happens when we let go of the illusion we have been clinging to that holds our conditioned reality in place.

Personal Survey on Conditioning

To get a glimpse of your own conditioned patterns, complete the sentences below as quickly as a response comes to mind. See if you can avoid the temptation to figure out what your response says about you.

Remember, only conditioning has an investment in your remaining ignorant of the ways you are programmed to respond. And what you don't know *can* hurt you. As you see more clearly how conditioning operates, you are increasingly able to make conscious choices about your responses in life.

I should_____

I must _____

People need to _____

It is important to_____

We simply have to _____

It is wrong to_____

It is not okay to_____

What matters is _____

They are_____

People don't_____

I can't stand people who_____

I hate it that_____

I just can't _____

The one thing I know to be true is_____

People who are cruel to animals are _____

Having children is _____

One's work is _____

Wealthy people are_____

War is _____

The world is the way it is because_____

Evil is _____

The right thing to do is_____

Poor people are _____

Security is _____

Relationships are_____

If you have_____you'll be okay.

I couldn't live without_____

I would die for _____

Remember: *You are eliciting these responses to better see the ways in which you have been conditioned. Your conditioning is not who you truly are. Please do not allow conditioning to use your awareness against you.*

Real Change

Here's an example of stepping out of the illusion of our conditioned reality. I am taught that it is selfish to consider myself. Ignoring and mistreating myself in the name of selfless-ness, I feel martyred, and I become self-righteous and manipula-tive. That approach, I decide, is not working; I am just going to be self-centered, letting myself do and have and be as I choose.

As a result, at first I find myself growing kinder, gentler, happier, and more generous. Then guilt begins to build. I am being selfish, and I know that is wrong. This time, however, I decide to explore the *process* of guilt rather than automatically believing I should feel guilty and returning to old patterns.

Another example: I withhold sweets from myself in the name of health and beauty. After a time, I become obsessive and resentful—and, yes, ugly. So I decide to let myself have as much as I want of anything I want to eat. At first, I eat a lot, but after a while, I often just take a bite or two of something and that's enough. More and more, I find myself relaxed about food. Increasingly, too, I am aware that wearing extra food on my body doesn't make me feel good. At the same time, I notice myself writing larger checks to agencies that provide food for hungry people around the world. As I relax about food, it seems I am more open to seeing a variety of relationships between people and food.

These are a couple of possibilities among endless possibilities. Once we release ourselves from the single-pointed focus that conditioning has on our awareness, we see that anything and everything is available to us.

You may think that this practice is hard, but it isn't. It's like painting a room, for which the preparation can be quite involved—masking the edges around windows, doors, light fixtures, and electrical outlets; spreading dropcloths over everything that hasn't been moved out; moving out everything else; then cutting in the corners. But once that's done, the actual painting is relatively easy. It's the same with this practice. Once we've completed the preparation, the actual work is a snap. And the preparation is not so much hard work as the shift to a different state of mind. Basically, it consists of the following:

- Having suffered enough to be open to something different

- Possessing enough clarity to realize that something different is possible

- Realizing that one does not know all that is possible

- Willingness to step into the unknown

- Courage to go up against the conditioning that will arise with growing awareness

Seeing into the Issue with Compassion

Now, here is an interesting question to raise—in a completely compassionate way, of course—in regard to the issue you are working with:

What is the payoff for my not [working for myself]?

Payoff is a term we usually hear in a positive context, meaning *reward*. That context keeps us from seeing that most of the payoffs we get in life are not at all what we would call positive. The payoff we usually get for our thoughts, our emotions, our behaviors, and our habits is feeling that we are bad/wrong/unworthy/alone/isolated/inadequate/unsuccessful. It can sound absolutely insane until one has the experience for oneself, but the real payoff is staying the same and surviving. How that works is illustrated in this story.

SAFETY IN DISSATISFACTION

Diane was never satisfied. She complained constantly. It hadn't always been that way. When she first met

Norm, she was sunny and charming, and when they first got together, she was happy and easy to please. As time went on, though, Diane began to find fault with more and more. Finally, Norm had had enough. He stayed later and later at work, didn't try to help Diane with her problems, and withdrew affection. They talked enough so that Diane knew exactly how Norm felt about her complaining, and she tried to change, but she couldn't. She would use expressions such as, "Old habits are hard to break," and "You can't teach an old dog new tricks," but underneath the clichés, she was frantic. Her marriage was at risk, and she seemed powerless to do anything about it.

❈ ❈ ❈

What Diane did not know, and could not see until she had spent a good deal of time watching herself in action, is that complaining was her childhood survival strategy. She came from an entire family of complainers. She certainly learned as she grew up that not everyone complained, and she learned to hide this tendency in order to be pleasing. But underneath the social facade, complaining *was* Diane: who she always had been, what she always had done, and how her family had been since before she could remember. Diane had no other orientation to life, and to give up her primary identification would feel like death. Diane loved Norm, but not more than her own survival, and her survival system would not loosen its grip on her life to save her marriage. If her complaining drove Norm away, on the level of her conditioning, that was acceptable—just one more thing to complain about. The payoff for Diane in complaining was that she got to keep in place the familiar world of her conditioning.

Payoff is important. When you want to know the answer to the question "Why?" about something in your life, look to see the result.

"Why do I keep dwelling on the past?" The payoff is that
when I'm dwelling on the past, I'm not in the present. That
means that there are no surprises. It's safe. I know how it
went and how it turned out.

"Why doesn't anything ever work for me?" Feeling like
a victim pays off in that I feel oddly superior to other
people—different, singled out by my persecution. And I
don't have to risk anything because I already know the
result will be things not working out.

"Why can't my mother and I get along?" Because then
I get to feel abandoned, unloved, and misunderstood,
and I get to take a lot of liberties to make up for what a
hard life I have.

Eventually, our "payoffs" can kill us. The doctor says, "Your
emphysema is progressing rapidly. If you don't quit smoking,
you're going to be dead in a year." "But I can't quit, Doc,"
wheezes the smoker. "How is this possible?!" you and I might
exclaim. "Doesn't this person get it? This is serious; this is literally life and death. Anybody in their right mind would do whatever it takes to quit."

Easy to say when it's someone else's struggle. "But my
issues aren't life and death," you and I might protest. In a moment
of honesty, though, we may question our certainty about that. If
we are not living the full, free, large lives that we want to live,
then we are denying life, and that is death. The biggest payoff for
most of us is comfort, ease, security, the known. We live our lives
so as not to "rock the boat," and in so doing, we have no resources
when the rough weather hits.

Here is another way of looking into our issue:

What would I have to give up in order to [work for myself]?

We're back to that negative payoff again, aren't we? I would have to give up my life as I have known it. I would have to give up struggling and failing and figuring this out and blaming myself and others and my whole comfortable, familiar way of being. The only way we will be able to do this, to give up what has been our payoff, is by bringing compassion to ourselves in this situation. A better way of expressing it, perhaps, is that we want to bring this situation, and the parts of us who suffer in it, into compassion where it can be embraced in total acceptance and understanding and love.

In the next chapter, we look more closely into the aspects of ourselves that depend for their survival on our not changing. And throughout—through this book and throughout our lives—we want to remember that compassion is called for every step of the way.

CHAPTER FIVE

SUBPERSONALITIES: Who Are We?

"Subpersonality" refers to one of many aspects of an individual, all of which share the designation "I." The idea that we are an aggregation of widely diverse identities that share a body has been around a long time in Eastern philosophy. The Buddha taught that each person is made up of such aggregates and that a constant, unchanging self is an illusion.

Subpersonalities reflect the various beliefs and assumptions we were required to accept as we grew up. Each family and each society has standards for manners, speech, behavior, cleanliness, attire, showing respect, work, roles, good taste, music, noise, beauty, and every other subject, situation, and issue known to humanity. The child must learn these and adapt appropriately. Each time the child's basic impulse collides with the standard for how things must be, a subpersonality is formed to carry out that adjustment.

To understand this better, let's explore in some detail how subpersonalities arise, quite naturally, in a child's development.

Survival .

The number-one job of a child is survival. To survive, certain basic needs must be met. Nature provides a wonderful balance of power in the dance of survival, which is often frustrating to those who are rearing children. While adults turn their efforts toward securing food, clothing, and shelter and establishing structure and order, the child's time, energy, and focus are totally committed to meeting survival needs. The adult is distracted and stressed by competing demands, but the child enjoys the power of single-minded attention. While social conditioning, in the form of messages from the adult, works to thwart much that is natural to childhood, the child is busy adapting. The collision of these cross-purposes can be delightful, but often it is unpleasant, sometimes to the point of cruelty and abuse.

When a child arrives in a social structure (usually but not always a family), it is essential for that child to secure its own place. In the beginning, an infant's physical demands automatically create that place; being fed, bathed, changed, held, and allowed to sleep constitutes its entire world.

Even in these relatively simple circumstances, the child is confronted with social conditioning. How often we hear people say, "You're going to spoil her if you pick her up every time she cries," and "He's just crying to get attention. Let him cry. It's good for him." Those are conditioned beliefs. Each of us holds just such conditioned beliefs about who children are and what they're doing. The difficulty is that we don't realize that; we think what we believe about the situation is true, and we react accordingly. In fact, we are operating out of a system of brainwashing.

As children grow, they begin the exquisitely subtle process of establishing their place in the world. To do that, they have to learn what works in the situations they live in. In their early years, children are doing everything possible to get the attention they need through pleasing the adults in charge. Over time it becomes clear that pleasing is not always possible, but the need for attention remains. Children quickly learn that *displeasing* is also a way to get attention, and it often works quicker and more reliably than pleasing does. So, if the family values togetherness, for example, being a loner can bring a certain amount of attention to a child.

The two sides of a duality appear—in the conditioned frame of reference—to be very different, even opposite. The way I see it, they are functionally the same. To take an example from adult life, let's say that in our family we have a conditioned standard about work. We don't necessarily say what that standard consists of, and it may never be consciously acknowledged, but we just *know* about work. We know who works hard and who doesn't. We know who is a good worker (and therefore a good person) and who isn't. Now, whether or not the family's standard is met *doesn't matter:* The true purpose of the standard is to control us. We are trapped in suffering because we believe, *deeply and thoroughly,* that one side of the duality is right and the other is wrong. *But that is not true.* I don't suffer because I am not a good worker, and my suffering won't end when I am a good worker. I suffer because I believe that my acceptability is *conditional,* that I am all right only if I am a particular way—usually a way that I am not!

Remember that agreement made by the child: *I will turn away from myself, give up my own authority, be who you want me to be, and you will meet all my needs.*

How a Child's Needs Are Met

I have worked with so many people over the years who say to me, mouth curled in disgust, "And I was just doing it for attention." Horrors! The ultimate in despicable behavior! We have been taught that to seek what we need is proof that we are bad, that we are wrong.

Children need attention. The constant, usually unspoken, question from a child is, "Am I here? Am I real? Am I okay? Will I survive?" The question is built into our biological being to ensure that the species will continue.

Responding to a child's need for attention is not the same as the "me-first-center-of-the-universe" tyranny of the tiny which is so popular today. Children do need to fit in, to be part of, to have a place, but that place does not need to be the center of everyone's world.

Most children, unfortunately, do not arrive in a world in which the adults are aware of their own social conditioning, let alone understand how that conditioning is passed along to a child. In fact, during the period that many parents see as the safest time in their child's life, the child is negotiating a path through dangerous terrain. If we take a step back from our own socialization, we can appreciate the irony. Because childhood is identified as a safe time, the potentially most damaging developments in a child's life remain unexamined.

A few years ago, I read that most automobile accidents occur within 25 miles of home. It could be argued, of course, that most driving is within 25 miles of home. But I can't help wondering if many of those accidents occur because we don't pay close attention to what is known, familiar, and therefore perceived as safe. If we attended as closely to what goes in on childhood as we do in situations we consider threatening, what would we see?

Let's imagine that you are a very small child. You need food and water, you need to be dry and comfortable, you need sleep and touch. Let's assume that for the first three or four months of your life, the people around you are willing and able to meet those basic needs. As we make that assumption, we have to keep in mind that you as a baby are operating from information that your parents don't have. You wake up and your stomach feels a particular way. Later you will identify that feeling as hunger, but for right now, there is just a sensation, and your response is to cry.

Your parents pick you up, change your diaper, make sure you are dry, and then being well-conditioned adults, look at the clock to see if you could be hungry. Nope. Baby ate two hours ago. Baby can't be hungry. Parents go through whatever they go through to try to help you out, but you are hungry, regardless of what the clock says. Odds are good that you will continue to cry until the clock says it's time for you to eat.

(Please remember that this is an example of the conditioning process, not an example of universal truth. Parents who subscribe to the "feeding on demand" school of thought are participating just as fully in the conditioning process, and conditioned results will follow from that opposite approach.)

We use this story simply to illustrate the process of social conditioning in action, not to find fault with parents. In this situation it is easy to understand that the parents can't tell what's going on inside the baby, and they subscribe to a belief system that tells them overfeeding an infant is not healthy. According to that belief system, a child cannot be trusted to eat as much as needed and then stop; the right way to eat is to eat a lot and then not eat for a certain amount of time and then eat a lot again. This may work for farmers or people in factories and offices who can eat only at specific times, but babies are not required to follow those rules—unless they have parents who hold that belief system. And are those rules appropriate for us once we're grown up? Most of us are terrified to go against what we have been taught in order to find out for ourselves. We choose our beliefs over our experience.

The Origin of Separateness

Let us look at this same process through a different lens. The newborn infant, as far as we can tell, does not experience itself as separate. As the baby grows and begins the process of adapting to the environment, the needs of the child often conflict with the belief systems of those providing its care. For example, Mother is attempting to feed Baby something it does not want to eat.

Mother pries the lips open and forces a little of the food into Baby's mouth. Out it comes, Baby's face scrunching up, the little body shuddering. Mother believes Baby must eat this food in order to grow and be healthy. Baby does not hold these beliefs and concentrates all its attention on not ingesting it. The competition is on. Mother persists, Baby resists. Tension grows in a battle of wills. Remember, all of this *means* a great deal to Mother; the well-being of her child, as well as her reputation as a parent, is riding on her successful completion of this task. Frustration grows as that little mouth stays clamped shut, and any food shoved in comes spraying out. Mother expresses her frustration through gritted teeth. Finally, Baby, perhaps sensing that this is getting out of hand, begins to shriek. Mother gives up and consoles the hysterical infant.

Have you put yourself in the mother's position? Can you recall feeling that frustrated, angry, and out of control? Now picture for a moment what it would be like to be the baby, having no idea what is going on, facing the force of that determined energy from the well-intentioned parent. Unfortunately, the baby has no way of knowing that this is a loving mother who only wants the best for her child. The baby feels the impact of all that parental will, aimed directly at it. How could the baby know that this is not a threat?

In examining the process that we all go through in our earliest years, I ask that you imagine yourself not as the parent but as the baby. The whole focus of your being is on survival: How can you get what you need and avoid being threatened by your caregiver? In that mealtime interaction between mother and infant, at least one subpersonality has been formed in the child. The need to eat what and when the body chooses has been rejected. The trauma of that rejection and the fear associated with the trauma each become a subpersonality, a permanent aspect of this child, a part of the survival system. Now, here is an interesting irony that beautifully illustrates how our conditioning works. When Baby refuses to eat, Mother concludes that what was offered needs to be altered in some way to make it more palatable. It does not occur to the mother that perhaps the baby is not hungry, or that food in a spoon instead of from a nipple needs more time to be introduced. Rather than coming to a simple, innocent conclusion, the parent consults her own conditioning and assumes the child's experience is the same as hers. Baby is not eating, Baby must not like the food. Maybe yes, maybe no. We assume that the baby holds opinions as we do, but opinions are learned as we grow older. Whatever might be going on with the food, Baby is certainly getting some lessons in how things work.

For instance, Baby has learned that "no" is not acceptable. We don't have a way to express concepts such as, "This is not the thing that works for me right now" that aren't loaded with *meaning*. It is difficult even to express what is actually happening without veering off into sixties-style pseudo-insight or New Age vagueness: "This is not what's happening now," or, "Right now, in this moment, the body does not have an agreeable response to that experience." Our conditioning finds it unacceptable for someone not to want something without a reason.

Baby is squarely up against this conditioning. It is time to eat. This is what medical science says a baby should eat, and baby has to eat it.

To combat this situation, Baby has developed a very effective weapon, screaming. In response, Mother goes into accommodating mode, adding sweetener or fruit or something else to the food, along with "Mmmmmm, good." We have a whole different relationship. In fact, we don't know why Baby now seems agreeable to eating the offered food. It could be that the Baby prefers sweets. It could be that some negotiating has gone on. It could be that mother is more agreeable about the whole issue. It could be that Baby became more comfortable with eating from a spoon. It could be something we would never think of. Here is the point: Instead of being freshly, authentically present in each moment, free of beliefs about what should and should not be, open to however this moment is, we usually drag in our whole conditioned survival system and superimpose it on each moment of life. Instead of being *here,* with all the potential and possibilities of *now*, we drag in our same old beliefs about "how it is" and turn possibility into the past.

This is what happened to us, via those who raised us, who were themselves conditioned in the very same way. This is what we do to ourselves, and it is what we pass along as we automatically, unconsciously attempt to condition others as we have been conditioned. Baby eats the food, at least most of the time, and Mother feels validated. "Baby has a sweet tooth."

So, who do we have so far? Subpersonality #1 is "not to be controlled about food." Subpersonality #2 is "scream when threatened." I bet there are more than a few of us who can recognize ourselves still living from those two subpersonalities at least some of the time.

There is another, even more fundamental, identity that has been formed in this exchange: the part who has been through the shock of having the caregiver refuse to meet a need. In fact, not only was the need refused but the caregiver was threatening and unreliable at the deep level of breaking the infant-caregiver agreement. Subpersonalities #3 and #4, perhaps, are ones who are frightened and unable to trust.

The Birth of Self-Hate

A little later, around the age of two or three, the child will have learned to identify with the authority figure who has failed to meet its needs. The survival behaviors created to meet the needs will still be employed, but the child will feel bad and guilty, believing that the treatment it received is warranted. "I am treated this way because I deserve it. I am bad and need to be punished. If I weren't bad, they wouldn't treat me this way." This is the birth of self-hate.

The next logical conclusion for the child is to try to be perfect. Many people I've worked with can remember the exact moment, usually around age six or seven, when they decided to be perfect. "If I'm perfect, if I do everything right, they won't need to get mad at me, and then they'll be happy and love me." This is the birth of the self-talk that maintains the self-hate.

The child has no choice other than this conclusion. Survival depends on the child taking all the blame. Why must it be the child's fault? Because the adults hold the child's survival in their hands—it is too threatening to the child to consider that the adult may be less than perfect. Later on, the child may give up the desire to be perfect when it becomes clear that achieving perfection is not possible and efforts in that direction go unrewarded.

We must keep in mind that a subpersonality is a defense mechanism, a survival strategy. With each obstacle along the way, a child accommodates, makes an adjustment. A need is not met, an essential desire is thwarted, and the personality splits. This can sound negative, like something to be avoided or overcome, but it isn't. This process of adaptation is completely natural. It is how survival is guaranteed.

Because each aspect of the personality was created and continues to exist in order to meet a core need, all subpersonalities are essentially good and helpful. The difficulty arises when as adults we are stuck with childhood reactions to current, adult situations. To gain insight into that situation, it is helpful to revisit the origins of our various identities.

❋　❋　❋

Johnny is coloring a picture. A parent or teacher or other authority figure walks by, looks at it, laughs, and says, "I guess Judy is the artist in the family." Johnny, crushed, throws his picture away and never does any- thing remotely artistic for the rest of his life. The person- ality formed to protect him is likely to be a macho fellow who thinks art is silly and strictly for girls.

❊　❊　❊

Judy wakes up in the night frightened by the sound of loud voices. She clutches her blanket, sticks her thumb in her mouth, and makes her way down the hall toward the sounds. When she enters the living room, which is full of party guests, her parents experience a variety of emo- tions, which, in some families, might include embarrass- ment. "Well, look who decided to join the party," her father jokes uncomfortably. The guests all turn toward Judy and laugh. Frightened, she runs crying to her room. The subpersonality who enables Judy to survive that event is shy and reserved. It is difficult for her as an adult to walk into a room filled with people.

❊　❊　❊

A subpersonality may be only a minute older than the one that preceded it. The child is going along in the unselfconscious world of childhood and receives a blow—physical, mental, emo- tional, or spiritual. The child who was there at that moment, open and receptive and vulnerable, disappears, a coping mechanism takes its place, and the adaptive subpersonality is created.

It is important to keep in mind that the child's response to a particular social demand can go in any direction. (For example, not all children would respond to the attention of grownups as Judy did; another child might adapt by seeking the spotlight.) If the family values responsibility above all else, a child may be ultraresponsible or completely irresponsible, but it is unlikely that the child will be neutral on the subject of responsibility. Defense systems are formed in reaction, and the reaction may be to ignore or rebel, but those are direct reactions. If an issue is vital in a child's surroundings, what is *not* an option is simply not noticing it.

Getting to Know Our Many Selves

The quickest, easiest way to determine if a behavior is coming from a subpersonality—if it is a conditioned behavior—is to notice how consistent it is. A consistent behavior is always conditioned.

For example, a person who is always late, or always on time, is operating out of conditioning and probably has an aspect of their personality who is in charge of time. The person who always overeats, always has a drink, always wears the same colors, always drives the same kind of car, is following conditioned, habituated patterns of behavior and has a particular identity who is evoked in response to particular life circumstances.

The sole function of a subpersonality is to meet the particular need that formed it. Subpersonalities are single-focused and have no awareness beyond their particular niche. For instance, a depressed subpersonality has no idea that other aspects of the personality are not depressed. I have worked with people who tell me one week that they are horribly depressed, and when I ask how long they've been feeling that way answer, "I've always been depressed." That is a true statement for that particular identity, but the previous week, or the next week, when another aspect of the person is talking with me, depression is nowhere in sight.

The identities we move in and out of include not only subpersonalities formed in early childhood but roles that emerge later—partner, parent, athlete, worker, and so on. Many subpersonalities can be involved in a single role. As a mother, for example, I can be warm and loving, stern and demanding, cranky, self-absorbed, distracted, resentful, and even childish. In fact, most subpersonalities can show up—appropriately or inappropriately—in any role.

Annie, Freddie, Cheryl, and Marshmellow

My first experience of subpersonalities was when, speaking to a dog with a thorn in its foot, I heard myself say in a high-pitched, unfamiliar voice, "Come here and let Annie take that out for you." Who? What? Pardon me, who is "Annie?" Not having any answers to that, I just filed the experience away. Later, with some practice in becoming aware of what goes on inside me, I realized that "Annie" is the part of me who interacts with animals and small children. She has never interacted with an adult; in fact, she is never present when adults are around. She appears in response to the defenseless. She is sweet, kind, and tender.

Freddie Fraidy Cat appeared when I began to make frequent long car trips. Before a trip, I would become sick and nearly paralyzed with fear that I would die in a car accident. I was not only terrified, I was embarrassed to have such an extreme reaction, and I was puzzled about it. To cover up those unacceptable feelings, I tried to make light of it by referring to that part of myself as "Freddie Fraidy Cat," but underneath there was contempt.

One day, as I was driving along counting my breaths, I had a sudden stab of memory. I saw myself years before, riding in another car, listening to the radio news report of the car wreck that killed my mother. After saying to me, "See you later," she had driven off on a trip she had made countless times—then died a horrible death—and I never saw her again. Reliving that loss and the way I had learned of my mother's being killed—how I screamed to the driver of the car I was in to stop, get me to a phone, help me, my mother was dead—I sobbed for that girl who was myself in that terrible situation. *Of course "Freddie Fraidy Cat" was afraid of driving on long trips:* Her whole world had been shattered in a car crash. As soon as I understood that, I held that terrified part of myself in my heart and vowed I would never again ridicule her for being afraid.

Putting all this into words suggests a degree of awareness that I didn't actually possess at the time. Now I have a framework for it: The part of me who felt separate and frightened was embraced in compassionate awareness. A compassionate presence, a wise mentor within me moved into the role of caregiver for that terrified girl. The girl who lost her mother was not going to be left alone with a part of me who wouldn't acknowledge her existence, didn't sympathize with her feelings, and found her embarrassing.

My two primary subpersonalities took a very long time to see, because they are like my skin, so "me" I couldn't see them. The first has the name I was born with, Cheryl, the name family and friends always called me—except for my mother, who called me Cheri.

I call Cheryl my eight-year-old hit-person. She carries a machine gun, and her motto is, "The only good adult is a dead adult." She's angry, she hates, she's violent. Cheryl could dismantle a house with a baseball bat—and would like to. Cheryl is the reason I became "Cheri" full-time.

I wish to be clear that all this rage and violence is only for those Cheryl considers "bad." Cheryl is a staunch protector of the innocent and defenseless. She loves children, animals, and old people as long as they are sweet and kind. But if someone is mean or cruel, even unwittingly or in jest, Cheryl wants them done away with. Needless to say, this has not won me any popularity contests. In fact, because of Cheryl, I grew up believing that I was a monster.

One evening, I was talking with a courageous and wise friend about Cheryl. She asked if I would be willing to do an introspective exercise that might help me get some perspective on this aspect of myself. As we proceeded, she asked me about Cheryl's purpose in my life. And, in a brilliant moment of insight, she asked, "Who does Cheryl protect?"

I saw a baby, just able to walk. When I was asked the baby's name, the answer was immediate: "Marshmellow." (Yes, "mellow.") Cheryl protects Marshmellow. Marshmellow was there before everything in the family got miserable—before my father developed a brain tumor; before he came home from the hospital, blind, unable to speak, and with a raging temper; before we had to be quiet all the time and never leave anything out of place that he might stumble over.

Marshmellow is sunshine and sweetness, she loves everyone, and she can't imagine that anyone would ever hurt her. Cheryl keeps her safe in a world no one can touch. I now work very hard to keep my friend Cheryl in a safe world where no one can touch her. I have an arrangement with Cheryl. If I'm not present, if I've lost conscious awareness of what is going on here and now, leaving Cheryl to make decisions about how life should be handled for maximum safety, I say nothing to her, regardless of the carnage that may result from her decisions.

My conditioning would have me go unconscious, act out from an identification with Cheryl (producing hurtful results for people around me), and then beat Cheryl (myself) for being such a hateful person. That's not helpful. Cheryl is a survival system, and no amount of punishment will make her different, although it can make her more convinced that her approach is necessary. Punishing Cheryl perpetuates the suffering. The only freedom lies in being present, conscious, and compassionately aware enough that Cheryl never needs to do her survival work.

Consider this analogy with parents and children. If I, as a parent, go away for the weekend and leave the kids at home alone, I cannot (if I have one shred of conscious awareness or common decency) blame the kids for doing the best they can do under whatever circumstances they find themselves in. They are, after all, kids. That's why they need responsible, conscious, present, aware, adults around to care for them. If I leave them to fend for themselves, I have to honor their decisions and choices. That may sound irrational and inflammatory, but I think a little reflection will prove its wisdom.

Working with Subpersonalities

People often ask two questions when confronted with the notion of subpersonalities: "Can you live without them?" and "How can I get rid of them?" (Please note that these questions themselves arise from our conditioning.)

Some schools of psychology work not toward getting rid of the subpersonalities, but toward integrating them, enabling them to "grow up" into one whole, unified personality. I have never felt the need to do anything with them except recognize and enjoy them. I think that our lives would be diminished by the loss of any aspect of ourselves. If I were to idealize anything, it would not be living without subpersonalities, it would be having free access to all the possibilities within a human being. Our difficulty is not with having various identities, it is the failure to recognize them for what they are, and, due to our lack of awareness, getting stuck in them. Many people are reacting from 2-year-old, 4-year-old, or 13-year-old survival strategies in situations that could definitely benefit from the presence of an adult!

While working with people and their subpersonalities, I have observed that those who attempt to get rid of an aspect of themselves are never successful. A subpersonality exists because someone tried to do away with a natural response. The subpersonality is an intelligent defense against anyone, including ourselves, permanently altering who we are. An attempt to eliminate a part of ourselves is thwarted by its "going underground." The person is simply unable to recognize the subpersonality and it goes right on doing its work of protecting them. Here are two examples.

PERSONAL BLIND SPOTS

Helen's view of herself is that she is a really nice person. She prides herself on this and will tell you about the many ways in which it is true. Unknown to Helen, those around her see her as aggressive, closed-minded, and difficult to please. How can this be? Wouldn't you think that Helen would notice herself behaving in these ways if in fact she did? What Helen notices, however, are the ways in which she meets her standards for being a really nice person. Behaviors that don't fit that image simply do not register.

❋　❋　❋

Ron considers himself a great family man, a loving husband and father. It is true that he is patient, kind, warm-hearted, and generous—until he isn't. Periodically, a dictatorial, intolerant tyrant takes Ron over, and during that reign, threatens his kids and humiliates his wife. Ron doesn't address this as a family problem because his need to view himself as a great family man prevents him from recognizing what he is doing.

❋　❋　❋

Helen and Ron both have strong, forceful aspects of their personalities that make sure their needs are met in their interactions with other people. They also have even stronger aspects of their personalities whose survival strategy is being the good, kind, loving person. These would be in conflict except for the fact that the individual is unaware of the unacceptable personality who is there taking care of them. (Prisons are full of people who are being punished because a crime was committed by a particular subpersonality, which, having fulfilled whatever need it was meeting, departed, leaving another aspect of the personality to take the blame.)

Everyone has subpersonalities. If someone says they don't, it's because a dominant personality is not allowing any others to be seen. If you have doubts about this, walk over to your closet and see how many folks have their clothes in there. Imagine the part of you that plays tennis putting on a tennis outfit and going to work. Imagine putting on your sexiest entertaining-at-home attire on the evening your parents come over for dinner. Can you recall a time when you arrived somewhere for some function and felt you were dressed all wrong? Have you ever reserved expensive tickets for an event and then when the time came, you wanted to stay home and wax the car? Can you picture all the people in your life coming to one party? Have you ever purchased something and looked at it the next day, wondering what possessed you? In addition to having their own wardrobes, subpersonalities have their own friends, interests, vocabularies, and worldviews.

When a person is stuck in trying to make a difficult decision, what is the underlying message in the common advice to "sleep on it"? Surely no one believes that the mere passage of time is going to alter the factors in the situation. I would suggest that there is an awareness that the individual is in the grip of a particular subpersonality, and that in the morning, it is likely that another subpersonality will be present, from whose perspective the problem will look different.

One subpersonality often sees the needs of others as a threat. Remember, each personality has been formed to meet a particular need, and not all of our needs are consistent. If I have a part of me who believes that it is necessary to have one other special person for security and another part who does not trust in intimate relationships, the road will be bumpy. Most of us have such conflicting needs along with the subpersonalities who are in charge of meeting them. My image of this is two little kids going down the road holding hands and punching one another. Part of me feels rich, another poor. Part of me is optimistic about the future; another part is terrified. One subpersonality is generous, the other stingy. One is disciplined, one is out of control. A part of me is tidy; another part is a slob. I want to start a family this week and to travel the world next week.

Opinions, convictions, worries, projections, fears, and judgments all come from subpersonalities. Only an identity who believes itself to be separate from everything else wants something other than what is.

Personal Survey on Subpersonalities

- Which part of you doesn't like where you are now in your life?

- Which part of you is concerned about the issue you've chosen to explore?

- Which part of you has done the work on this issue that has been done so far?

- Which part of you decides what in that process has worked and what has not?

- Which part of you sabotages your efforts and stops you from having what you want?

Remember: *You are seeking awareness in this area to better see the ways in which you have been conditioned. Your conditioning is not who you are. Please do not allow conditioning to use your awareness against you.*

Here is a story I heard about two subpersonalities and the illusion of control.

GEORGE

I am constantly upset that my life feels out of control. There are two subpersonalities that immediately come to mind around this issue. One is the Idealist. He has an idea about how everything in life should be. Indeed, his favorite pastime is telling me about how life should be, and his next favorite pastime is telling me that I should be living up to these ideals that he has. I should be a devoted, romantic, caring, attentive husband. I should be a hard-working, creative, diligent, self-starting employee. I should be a hard-working, conscientious, knowledgeable homeowner.

The counterpart of the Idealist is the Free Spirit. The Free Spirit is completely focused on freeing me from every responsibility: job, marriage, homeownership, and impending fatherhood. He's always thinking about when I can get time to myself. When will I get off work? When will my wife go to bed so I can watch TV by myself? When will the chores be done?

The Idealist is the one who feels that he has the problem. He's really upset that everything seems so out of control. As I think about this, though, something interesting occurs to me. The Idealist thinks that everything would be okay if only I were different. If I had more willpower, more initiative, more courage, more whatever, I'd be happy. The Free Spirit thinks everything would be okay if only circumstances were different. If I were rich enough to be able to retire right away and just travel, I'd be happy. Both parts don't like where I am now, but one looks at the problem as being on the inside, and the other sees the problem as being on the outside.

It's a bit unsettling to think about "who" is doing this awareness process. I assumed it was just "me." But then I guess the whole idea of "me" is one of the biggest assumptions that we need to question in developing awareness.

When I think of how seriously I take this spiritual work—and I don't mean that in a good way—I begin to suspect that the Idealist is behind some of it. The Idealist is a very, very serious guy. I think it appeals to him to have this work that involves "fixing" some issue that's "wrong" with me. He has me on a very disciplined schedule, trying to make sure I do what is needed every day to fix me.

I think both the Idealist and the Free Spirit are sabotaging me in their different ways. The Idealist is too busy figuring out how I can be perfect to allow me to have much real interaction with the world, and the Free Spirit is telling me that I can't enjoy anything that involves responsibility. It is as though they are conspiring to keep me a step removed from my life.

❋   ❋   ❋

My response to George: Bingo! I think you're on to something. But let me make a really obvious point that our conditioning causes us to overlook. Neither of these guys has a body.

Neither of these guys is real. These are illusory pieces of conditioning that talk to you about what is wrong with you and your life. They don't have lives—how did they get to be authorities on yours?

That is a critical point to consider. If your neighbor, relative, or friend said the kinds of things to you that these illusions are saying to you, you would wonder why they were talking to you like that. What business would it be of theirs? And your friends, relatives, and neighbors at least are real enough to have bodies!

We get bamboozled every time, because when a voice inside our head starts talking to us, we just *assume* it is coming from a real person and we believe everything it says. One careful observer recently mentioned how silly the voices sound when we actually pay attention to what they say. Add to the absurdity of their messages the fact that they are just mental formations, and it is clear that the suffering they cause is absolutely unnecessary.

Seeing into the Issue Through an Awareness of Subpersonalities

Let's examine the issue we're working with through the lens of subpersonalities.

Who would I be if I [worked for myself]?

I have no idea who I would be if I worked for myself. In fact, I cannot even picture it except in vague, general kinds of ways. Working for myself has been a carrot that, for the most part, has kept me in a place of dissatisfaction that I have believed would lead to what I want. Being dissatisfied, thinking, fantasizing, blaming, criticizing, judging, rationalizing—that's what I *do*. That is, in addressing this issue, I have approached it only as one or another subpersonality who wants something other than what is. Who will I be if I have no need to do that anymore?

A fear of losing identity in this way was overcome by the person who tells this story:

DESTINY

Ed grew up in a poor neighborhood. Both his parents worked, and still they barely had enough to get by. There was a lot more wanting than having in their household from the moment Ed, the youngest of five children, was born. The deprivation extended beyond material things to care, support, and encouragement.

Ed knew for as long as he could remember that someday it would be different for him. He knew that it was a mistake for him to be in a family like his—he wasn't that kind of person—poor. He was destined for better things and knew he would do whatever was necessary to achieve his "real" lifestyle. Ed worked hard, got scholarships and loans for his education, held part-time jobs, and studied to the point of exhaustion. When he graduated from college, he took a good job and began to work his way up in the company.

When Ed came to me for spiritual guidance, he had achieved the success he desired—money, possessions, an attractive wife, a beautiful home in a posh neighborhood. He was an important person who could have anything he wanted, except the one thing he truly wanted: happiness. It had not occurred to him that poverty is not synonymous with unhappiness and money does not guarantee happiness.

Ed approached life as most of us have been taught— as a series of things to do, rather than as a process to be. What he grew to realize is that throughout his struggle to become someone different, he continued to cling to his identity as a poor kid. His hatred of being poor drove his struggle to be someone else. Without that poor kid and his hatred of poverty, he believed, he would have no inspiration to strive. Of course, Ed was not aware of this process until he noticed that even with all the new externals in place, he was still that poor kid.

※　※　※

This could seem like some sort of cruel joke that life is playing—your reward for working hard and being good is that you don't get what you want—but Ed would not agree at all. What he has learned is that he can finally take care of that unhappy little kid. Did that child really want money? No, he wanted to avoid what he associated with poverty, a lack of care and nurturing. Each one of us can take responsibility for providing for ourselves that which we've always felt we lacked. Ed knows that now, and instead of his life being a miserable disappointment, he is starting all over with the happy task of making a little boy who felt left out and unloved—himself—feel included and cared for.

In the past few years, the whole notion of the "inner child" has taken some pretty hard hits. Popular culture has taken up the language, comics have made jokes, and the whole concept has been trivialized. Be that as it may, anyone who has spent any time at all in introspection or observation of others knows that each stage of development that we have gone through from infancy is still with us. We try to hide that fact, and have laws and social rules to attempt to suppress it, but the feelings and behaviors remain. We've all seen the adult descend into the temper tantrum of a toddler when thwarted in some significant way. We know what's it like to be attempting a grown-up activity and find ourselves feeling as overwhelmed and inadequate as we felt on the first day of school. Most of us have times when we feel like an insecure, socially inept preadolescent.

Part of taking responsibility for oneself is taking responsibility for one's selves. As we practice awareness, we learn to view ourselves with compassionate understanding rather than harsh judgment. Instead of hating the part of himself who still feels poor and uncared for, Ed can learn to be the kind, caring, compassionate mentor he needed so desperately but never had as a child.

In the next chapter, we will explore an important way to tune in to just such parts of ourselves.

CHAPTER SIX

LISTEN:
Tuning in to Self-Talk

A ll day long, our subpersonalities "talk" to us; this is what is known as "self-talk." If you don't actually attend to what is going on in your mind, it is easy to assume you are "just think- ing." But as soon as you begin to pay attention, you can hear the different personalities talking about themselves and their views of the world.

One of the first voices you may hear is that of the "Judge." The Judge is the identity formed by that long-ago decision to be perfect. The logic behind the Judge is that if I can monitor and punish myself before anyone else does, no one else will need to. For most people, the Judge is a full-time, life-time appointee with no plans to retire. It is a painful picture: a young child within us (remember that the Judge was formed at age six or seven) pass- ing judgment on even younger children within us, who accept whatever criticism and punishment the Judge hands down.

As we sit still and learn to pay closer attention, we become aware of the intricate, complex structure that is our conditioning, and we start to see how it is held in place. I find it fascinating that as a culture we have such a fear of brainwashing since, as far as I can tell, the system of social conditioning is the very blueprint for brainwashing. Over and over we are told what is not true until we believe it. Our programming is complete when we have learned to tell all those untrue ideas to ourselves.

Most of us are far away from the source of our internal voices. We don't remember where, when, and how we learned to talk, listen, and respond to ourselves as we do. Many people don't hear their self-talk, and others hear it but don't realize what it is. Nevertheless, we do talk to ourselves, and we can learn to listen to that talk as a way of increasing our awareness of how we operate. See if you can imagine a conversation such as this going on inside your own head.

Why did I wear this? I feel so uncomfortable.

I wish they were serving alcohol.

Why did you say that?

What am I doing here?

Hmm, I wonder who that is. What an arrogant so-and-so he is.

Will this never end?

Why don't you ever say anything intelligent?

I wonder how much it costs to get a flight to Hawaii.

What's the date today? I think I forgot to pay the mortgage.

It's the 14th, you idiot, that's why we're attending this disaster.

Oh, come on—I love parties. Why can't you ever relax and have fun?

I need to get to the bank first thing in the morning.

Anyone who has ever attempted to meditate will tell you that this kind of talk goes on incessantly. Some voices talk in terms of "I" and some in terms of "you." We are receiving constant information that tells us who we are, what we like, what is important, what we should be doing, what others should be doing, how others are, and how they should be—in other words, we have a nonstop voiceover of repeated beliefs, assumptions, and opinions that keeps our conditioned world in place.

Hearing Voices

I encourage you to pay attention to everything that is being said inside your head. It's a quick way of getting to know aspects of yourself that you are probably unaware of. In my on-line workshops, I invited people to report on what their voices were saying about the issue they had chosen to work with. These two responses are typical of the kinds of things we may hear often if we listen closely:

What makes you think you know anything about this? You'll make a fool of yourself. Do you think anyone cares what you have to say?

Why would you have to pick fear of death as your issue? What a morbid subject! You're really going to bum everyone out.

In terms of content, the reports on voices covered quite a gamut. A woman who was working with jealousy related this account.

CLAIRE

What makes it difficult for me is that I lose myself in fear, doubt, and dread of abandonment. The voices tell me contradictory things. "Jealousy is biologically based. It comes from your animal nature. You can't help it." And, "It's wrong to be jealous. You should heal this issue as part of keeping your husband. You should be kind, loving, trusting, completely accepting, and so secure in yourself that you're not worried about him." The voices call me evil, vindictive, weak, bad, spiteful, insecure, clinging, enslaved, possessive, co-dependent, and childish.

Here is someone else's report of internal verbal abuse.

PAM

I suppose my issue is being a weenie. I'm weak. I get so insecure—paranoid, really—and I complain and whine. I can't seem to help it. The voice that says, "You see, he/she/they hate you" is so believable. I'm constantly scanning for proof of being hated. That either drives me away from people—I leave them before they leave me—or it drives people away from me because trying to confront this in myself makes me a whiner, not someone people want to be around.

The voice tells me that I should be strong and have faith that the feeling will pass and keep my mouth shut. If only I could be content and assume that the other person is just going through something temporarily and will snap out of it, instead of thinking it must be because of me, something I've done wrong. If only I could relax, be confident, and quit scanning for proof (it takes so much energy!).

But I get sucked into it, and I just can't resist. It's a cycle of self-battering: I try to keep a lid on my feelings, pressure builds, I act out, I feel better/feel worse, I beat myself up, then I start over, trying to keep a lid on it. The voices call me a loser, a failure, and an idiot. They say things like: "Nobody likes you," and "You'll always be alone" and "I hate you." I should keep my mouth shut, and when I can't, they beat me up. I try to hide to minimize the ammunition the voices can get their hands on. I think I'm a weenie/insecure because they have me so convinced that nobody likes me—obviously, there is something wrong with me.

Another observer reported:

STEVE

While balancing my checkbook today, it became apparent that I had once again not paid enough attention to my account balance on a daily basis and had come up a bit short. This is usually a Very Big Deal for me, a perfect occasion for self-hatred. The usual voices started to come up: "You did it again, genius. When are you ever going to learn? You really are an idiot." This is usually followed by depression, possibly an urge to do harm to myself in some way, and definitely a sudden drop in energy.

This time I said to myself, "Well, am I going to listen to the voices of conditioning and beat myself up, or not?" I decided to let the conditioned thoughts go, and then I went on with the business of balancing my checkbook and enjoying the rest of my day.

It occurred to me that while there is no doubt that I can pay closer attention to my checking account on a regular basis and therefore avoid this situation in the future, self-hatred and self-abuse were not going to solve my financial difficulties for me.

❉   ❉   ❉

And this came from another:

JASON

I have three distinct voices in my head telling me all kinds of things about being out of touch with my feelings (which is the issue I'm working with). Fear tells me that I can't look at my feelings because there's something scary there, and if I look, it will either drive me crazy or I'll start crying and won't be able to stop. It's telling me to just go on as before, and it'll sort itself out. Ego tells me that I need to get in touch with my feelings pronto so that I can deal with them swiftly and get balanced and centered, and then won't I be someone special! It tells me to try everything and to loudly announce to everyone how introspective I am in the process. Compassion tells me that I can look at whatever comes up and that I won't abandon myself, and just to take my time and to do whatever I need to support myself.

Fear tells me that having this problem means there's something really wrong with me. Ego tells me that having this problem means I'm a control freak and haven't been handling things correctly. Compassion tells me that having this problem is simply a symptom of a year of extreme external crises and my need to hold everything together, and that now that the crises have passed and my external life is resolved and peaceful, I have time to process the feelings that I've been suppressing for so long. Ego tells me that I'm not superman after all if I can't even handle looking at my feelings just because a few things in my life are crazy.

Fear tells me that I'm slipping and am not as strong as I think I am. Compassion tells me that I'm aware that I'm not aware of my feelings, and that this is a good step toward knowing myself. It tells me that I tried suppressing my feelings as a means of protecting myself and my family, but that it didn't work out very well, and that I'll learn from this and do it differently next time.

Funny—just saying that I'm going to pay close attention to what the voices are saying is making them very quiet right now.

Detecting Self-Hatred

The process of social conditioning, as it reinforces the ability to experience oneself as separate from life, creates the illusion that as a separate self, one must do whatever is necessary to survive. Conditioning also provides the tools—a set of beliefs and assumptions, various subpersonalities, and the ability to project our conditioned views onto the world at large, along with a constant tape loop (the voices in our head that talk us into and through our programmed reality)—to ensure the survival of our egocentrically conditioned identities. The way we are locked into this system is by being taught that if we don't follow the program exactly, we are bad and wrong and will be punished. We are taught to fear and hate ourselves when we aren't the way we are supposed to be and don't do what we are supposed to do.

I wish I had a dollar for every time someone has said to me, "Well, you just don't know me—there really *is* something wrong with *me*," or "Self-hate? No, I don't hate myself. Maybe I'm a little hard on myself sometimes, but hate? Naw, that's too strong a word." I suppose it *is* too strong a word, unless one is perfectly at ease with being called bad, wrong, stupid, lazy, ugly, and a loser. For anyone who doesn't think those voices are coming from self-hate, it may be helpful to ask yourself, "Would I speak that way to a child I love? Would I allow a stranger to speak to me in that way?"

Most of us quickly realize that we would not tolerate this kind of treatment from anyone. So why do we tolerate it from the voices inside our heads? Because these voices have been there for as long as we can remember. Because we think these voices are who we are. Because we think they are protecting us and we are afraid to be without them. Because we think of them as the voice of truth—the voice of "God"—and we are terrified that if we reject them, we will be punished. Because we are afraid of ourselves without them.

I recently asked people in a workshop, "What is a friend? How do you know when a person is a friend?" Some of their responses:

A friend . . .

. . . is a person I feel safe with
. . . doesn't make fun of me
. . . wants to see me happy and successful
. . . can communicate easily

. . . can laugh and share humor
. . . requires no censoring, no masks
. . . is a good listener
. . . is understanding
. . . is compassionate
. . . is totally accepting
. . . is helpful, tolerant, and respectful
. . . is someone I do things with
. . . is someone I like
. . . shares intimate secrets
. . . doesn't blame
. . . doesn't judge
. . . strikes a balance between giving and receiving
. . . forgives
. . . knows that I'm awesome
. . . loves me for who I am
. . . looks out for me
. . . gives me slack
. . . loves me unconditionally
. . . shares interests
. . . is someone I can trust

People are afraid to discount the voices because they might have something valuable to say, but this list can be a useful reality check. The next time a voice in your head is talking to you about who or how you are, ask yourself, "Is this how a friend would speak to me? Would I call a person a friend who treats me in this way?" If the answer is no, you can stop listening to that voice and reconsider its role as an internal authority on your life. If the answer is yes, go to a person who loves you as unconditionally as possible, and ask that person to give an opinion as to whether or not the voice is something you want to be friendly with.

Notice whether the voices are speaking from "I" or from "you." In most cases, the voice is saying, "You are bad/wrong," and I am the recipient of the self-hatred. Even though it is all happening inside "me," it doesn't seem as if I'm calling myself those names. I am the listener, not the speaker. When I am speaking in the "I" voice, I am still the recipient of the information, with the difference being that now I am conditioning myself, rather than having someone else condition me. "I shouldn't be so weak. I shouldn't be useless." I am telling myself what I have been told and believe I still need to learn.

It is easy to hear in this the early social conditioning of childhood. A child hears a voice of authority giving direction on how to be and what it means about the child if the child doesn't comply. The child, needing to survive in a large, scary world, begins to internalize the information. "I need to be this way. I need to do that."

If you want to have a direct experience of this process in action, position yourself to overhear a group of three- to four-year-olds playing "life." One will be the dad, one will be the mom, and the other hapless victims will be the children. After observing for a while, you might say to yourself, "Surely no one has said those things to those children. Surely they are not treated like that." This is a sobering moment if you happen to be the parent of one of those children. Your reaction will be more like, "I have never treated that child like that! I have never said those things!" True, perhaps, but here is the essential point: *That's what it sounds like to the child.*

Listen as we talk to one another. Listen to the impatience, the intolerance, the judgment in our tone of voice, in our inflections. Listen to one adult explaining something to another adult. Listen to the way we talk to children. Listen and try to imagine what message you would be getting if you had no idea how life works.

For most of us, the only time we *become* the voice of self-hatred is when our conditioning is turned outward and projected onto others. If we have an opportunity to vent our frustrations on someone else—in traffic, toward a stranger we read or hear about, or talking to a friend about people at work—we can hear the judgments that are usually leveled at ourselves internally being directed toward someone else. Many people report that it feels good, it feels powerful. We're told we are wrong so often that it can feel satisfying to make someone else more wrong than we are!

Of course it doesn't *really* feel good, because we're taught to feel guilty about treating people badly. Even when we feel justified and righteous, there is often that nagging little spot of feeling worse for having felt better at someone else's expense. For many people, the time when this process feels the worst is when we hear ourselves do to our children what was done to us. In fact, I've talked with many people who finally found the willingness to bring conscious awareness to their internal process when they realized they had *become* their mother or their father.

We have been taught to believe that we can make something go away by hating it, when, in fact, hating it is what keeps it in place. *If we never attended to a particular issue again, it would go away.* Technically, it wouldn't go away so much as it would cease to be there, because the only thing holding it in existence is the resistance that conditioning brings to it in the form of convincing us we need to do something about it. "I have a problem. I am this way. I should be that way. I feel this, but I should feel that. I do this, but I should do that. The way I am makes me a bad person. I should be the other way so I will be a good person." This is the hell of duality. This is the creation and maintenance of suffering.

A Conversation about Self-Hate

Cheri (C) and a friend (F) are talking about the process of egocentric social conditioning as applied to a specific issue:

C: So, what issue are you working on?

F: Oh, the same old issue I always work on—going unconscious in the evening and drinking and eating too much of the wrong stuff.

C: So, what is the issue?

F: I eat junk food and drink beer and then wake up in the night with the voices pummeling me.

C: So, the problem is . . . ?

F: There is no centered presence to keep me from going unconscious and indulging in self-hating behaviors.

C: But what is the problem?

F: There is no one who is centered. . .

C: May I give you a hint?

F: Sure.

C: There may be no centered presence there, but what *is* there?

F: [Pause] Someone who judges what I should and should not do.

C: Exactly. Some part of you is holding a standard about how you should be, and you aren't meeting it. If that part weren't there, would there be a problem?

F: Well, maybe there wouldn't be a problem, but wouldn't I just go on eating and drinking too much until I died?

C: First of all, I doubt if eating tortilla chips and a bowl of ice cream and drinking a couple of beers is going to do nearly as much damage as the self-hate does. Here is the part that interests me. What might your evening look like if you didn't drink and eat those things? What if, for instance, you were feeling lonely. . . ?

F: That is exactly what I'm feeling.

C: And I bet a voice comes in pretty quickly following

that awareness to convince you that "a nice cold beer would go good right now." But what if you just stayed with that part of you that is lonely? What if you didn't have a drink to numb her feelings or eat so much food that there was no room for her to be there? I suspect what would happen is that you would get to know her, turn your attention to her, spend time with her, and soon neither one of you would feel lonely or have a need to numb yourself to one another's presence. What happens instead is that conditioning causes you to run to the refrigerator (away from that lonely person) and then beats you up for having done what it encouraged you to do in the first place. That's always the case. Self-hate talks you into doing something and then beats you up for doing it.

F: [laughing] "So what's the problem?" I've been see-ing the problem as having no discipline, but the real problem is believing the voices of self-hate.

C: Yes, you could say that—if you really want this to be a problem at all. There is an alternative. You might consider viewing the whole thing as your very best opportunity to see through egocentricity's ploys, to wake up, and to end suffering.

On occasion, after hearing an exchange like this, someone will ask me a question along the lines of, "But what if your friend had been shooting up heroin or abusing a child—would you still tell her that that's probably not doing as much harm as the self-hate?" In other words, isn't self-abuse what keeps us from abus-ing drugs or people? The answer is emphatically, unequivocally, *no*. Self-hate does not prevent abuse; *self-hate is the cause of abuse.* Those who are victimizing others are doing it precisely *because* they themselves feel victimized.

The old story says it best. The boss yells at the worker, who goes home and yells at his wife, who slaps the child, who kicks the dog. (Next we'll be hearing about a dog who, for no apparent reason, attacks a neighbor.)

The voices of conditioning will go into overdrive to get you to stop doing this work, to prevent you from becoming more aware, and to make you stop watching them. See if you can commit to letting yourself go through this process regardless of what conditioning says or does. Suffering happens in the dark. With this work, you are turning on the light. You can expect the voices to escalate, so it is beneficial to keep in mind that the fact that people are yelling doesn't mean they have valid points to make.

Hungry Ghosts

The "hungry ghost" is a Buddhist image for egocentric conditioning. The hungry ghost has a huge belly and a very long neck that tapers into a tiny head with a nearly imperceptible mouth. This creature feeds on the energy of suffering, going through life frantically trying to poke enough "food"—the energy of dissatisfaction, criticism, misery, pain, punishment, self-hate—through that minuscule aperture to satisfy its enormous belly. The hungry ghost represents the insatiable appetite of egocentricity. Keep in mind that this creature does not consume the suffering itself (that would make it a handy pet to have around!), but feeds on the energy that attends suffering. That means that egocentric conditioning must keep us in a continuous state of suffering to maintain a constant source of sustenance.

Being on the horns of a dilemma—flipping from one side of a duality to the other—puts us in the ideal position for the hungry ghosts to feed on us. We have a choice between this or that, and we decide, "I'll do this" (lots of energy, the hungry ghosts eat the energy until it's gone). And then we say, "Oh, no! This was a mistake—I need to do that" (lots of energy, the hungry ghosts feed on the energy until the energy is gone). "Oh, no! What a mistake"—on and on and on, ad nauseam. Everyone—that is, the hungry ghosts of egocentric conditioning—is well fed except the poor person who is trapped in this duality.

Let me explain in different words. There is a sense of a "you" that is present when everything else falls away. The intelligence, the awareness, the sensitivity, the nonseparateness, the life force that animates you, the known which cannot be understood, is apparent when all the yammer of social conditioning stops for a split second. For that instant, there is the awareness of nonseparate presence. (You have to leave that presence in order to talk about it, to have a relationship with it, to make it an object to which you as a separate self are the subject.) That's who you experience as "you" when the self-hating, self-judging voices of conditioning don't have you by the throat. Those hungry ghosts want you to suffer because they're parasites living on the emotion/energy of suffering that is generated by convincing you to believe that you're what the voices say you are rather than who you truly are.

Here are several types of things that the voices of conditioning might be saying to you now about the issue you have chosen to work with. Let's see if we can figure out what's really going on.

You picked a bad issue. Your issue isn't as good/smart/ deep/significant as other people's.

Any voice that is talking to you is conditioned. Listen to it so you will know the kinds of things conditioning tries to convince you of, but do not believe it. The most intelligent and helpful response to the conditioned voices is, "Is that so?" or something equally noncommittal such as, "Hmmm." Don't let them pull you in. Sit tight and just notice. Notice your tendency to get hooked in.

*This is something you shouldn't talk about. Keep quiet so
no one will know what an awful person you are.*

When a child is being sexually abused, the abuser convinces
the child that no one must ever find out what's going on because
if anyone finds out, everybody will know how bad the child is and
the child will be punished. Is that true? Is that what everyone will
find out? Or will everyone see the abuse for what it is, side with
the child, protect the child, remove the abuser, and support the
child in being free of the abuse?

The latter is what we're doing here. And the best thing each
of us can do is "spill the beans." Tell it all. "The voices say . . ."
"Now they're saying . . ." "They're threatening me with. . ."
"They say I'm _____ for doing this work." Be a whistle-
blower, and prove to yourself that the only power the voices have
is the power you give them. Remember the most significant point
to keep in mind about the voices of conditioning: *They have no
body.* The only things they can do to you are what they can talk
you into doing to yourself. They're feeding on your fear of them.

*My problem is that . . . well, no, actually, it's more
like . . . but really I think it's that I'm . . .*

Your issue keeps switching on you, slip-sliding away. About
the time you wrap your mind around it and try to pin it down so
you can take a look at it, it oozes off into something else.
Suggestion: Do a peaceful sit-in. Let conditioning know that you
are going to disregard everything it says if it doesn't tell you
specifically, exactly what the issue is. If this were a court of law
and the prosecution told the judge that the crime is murder, but—
well, not really murder, more like armed robbery, except nothing
was stolen, so maybe just armed assault, although without a
weapon—pretty soon the judge would throw the case out
of court.

The reason that the problem keeps shifting is that if it stayed constant, you could address it. Conditioning keeps itself a moving target. It can always make you feel bad because you can't solve a problem it won't state. As I point out in *That Which You're Seeking Is Causing You to Seek*, the way you can tell if a problem is real or imaginary is that if it doesn't have a solution, it's imaginary.

Here is a little exercise I encourage you to do if you are having difficulty "making a decision." The voices start making a case for one side of the issue. Perhaps you decide that saving some money each week is a good thing to do. As soon as you decide to do it, the voices kick in with the reasons you should do the opposite. You begin to be convinced that they're right after all; okay, I won't save money. Then come the voices from the other side. "But really maybe you should . . ." After you have been hammered back and forth for a while (but before you give up and lose interest in the conflict) a voice says, in a tone of disgust, something along the lines of, "What a loser you are. You can't even make a simple decision."

Can you hear the munch, munch of hungry ghosts? Before the chomping gets too loud, try this: Go through the two sides of the argument once, so you know what your choices are, then designate one side of the duality as A and the other as B. If this is the first time you've done this exercise, choose A, in a totally arbitrary, no-logical-rationale kind of way. The next time you find yourself on the horns of a duality, choose B. No second thoughts; just choose B. Next time, A; the time after, B. It is the most perfect way to watch the voices of conditioning go crazy! This might not sound like conditioning's idea of a compassionate spiritual approach, but conditioning has spent plenty of time driving us crazy, and a little turnabout-is-fair-play can't hurt. Furthermore, it is very, very effective in seeing exactly what's going on.

Your problem is real (whereas some other people's problems are totally imaginary), and it's very serious, and all this examination of it isn't going to change that.

You can begin to question that by considering your friends' beliefs about their own issues and comparing your experience of them.

He thinks he's a loser. I don't know why—I think he's a great guy who is too hard on himself.

She thinks she's not that intelligent, but I think she's bright and funny.

He thinks he should have more control. I think he needs to relax!

She thinks she's a failure, but I admire what she's done in life.

Unless you're determined to hold on to the delusion that you are the only exception to the universal principle of inherent adequacy (that we are equal to our lives)—unless you want to believe that while we each see ourselves as more unworthy than everyone else, *you really are* less worthy than everyone else—you will begin to realize that everyone's voices try to convince them that they are uniquely unworthy. That's why egocentricity fights so hard against an awareness practice. It might tell you that it doesn't want you to have to face how bad you are, but the real reason it fights is that you are going to see through the scam that ego is running and release yourself from its grip.

The Worst

I run across a lot of people who are playing the "I'm the worst/most hopeless/most unworthy person in the world" game. It is exceedingly hard to be the best; most of us gave up the hope of being the best long ago, although we didn't stop competing. What many competitors found is that the position of the worst seems available—and egocentricity, the illusion of a separate self, desperately wants to be special.

Egocentricity must be the center of the universe all the time, center stage every moment, in order to get the amount of energy put into it that it needs to survive. (It is for this reason that most people find boredom to be the most terrifying state of all.) How can egocentricity do this? By comparison. "I am different." But that's obvious; not a lot of charge there. "Yes, but I shouldn't be different." Ah, big charge in that *shouldn't*. I *should* be thin and rich and famous and gorgeous and successful and humble and sweet and kind and selfless and generous and good and unobtrusive and of service and independent and responsible and brave and compassionate and helpful and clever and . . . please fill in some of your own personal favorites.

But I am not all these things all the time. If I were, then I would be good and right and lovable. Since I am not, my identity becomes the one that is not the way it should be, the one that is bad, wrong, different, not able to fit in—*separate.*

How does this process of being the "odd person out" go undetected? Because our talk throws us off the scent. For instance, I say to you that all I want is to be happy, but I just can't seem to be, for some reason or other. You suggest to me that I try a certain way of solving the problem. "No, that won't work for me." Well, how about this other approach? "No, I've tried that." Well, maybe you could do this. "No, that's just not for me." Well, have you thought about such-and-such? "No, I haven't considered that, but I'm sure it wouldn't work." What is really going on here?

Let's consider an analogy. I call the mechanic to start my car. I am frantic. I'm late to a really important appointment. My whole future is hanging in the balance. The mechanic arrives and identifies the problem as a weak battery. "No problem," the mechanic states confidently. "All you need to do is put the car in second gear, put in the clutch, turn the ignition to 'on,' and when I push you and get you rolling pretty good, pop the clutch out and the car will start."

"Well, I don't know," I say. "What if that's not the problem? I don't understand why what you're suggesting would work."

The mechanic's response might be something along the lines of, "Do you want to start the car or not? If you're an expert in this subject, why haven't you started the car? Why call *me?*"

As crazy as it sounds, my *identity* has become: "It won't work for me." If something worked for me, then I would have to give up being the worst, most hopeless, most unworthy person, the one who is inherently and irredeemably flawed. I would have to stop the habit of comparing in order to lose the contest and feeling right when I see I've proved once again that, "It's true, it just won't work for me." Maybe others can end suffering, but not me. I really want to, but there's just something wrong with me. Yep, deep down I'm flawed.

Egocentricity breathes a huge sigh of relief and surveys its domain at the center of the universe. "The problem is not with the problem; the problem is with *you*. If you would just do that right thing and get some control over yourself and your life, there would be no problem."

Conditioning is using control to control you. If you want to keep people busy, give them a task to do that cannot be done, and convince them they must do it. If they're convinced that it can be done and they must do it, they will probably never question the original assumption that it is possible. Being in control of life is an illusion. There is no such thing as control. It doesn't exist. Never has, never will. Egocentricity puts you in charge of getting control and itself in charge of monitoring your efforts, and you belong to it. Ego says, "When you possess this thing that does not exist, you will be all right, you will be a good person, and you will be allowed to enjoy your life." Sounds to me like a pretty good description of hell.

So what does a person do? Get interested in the process. Get interested in *how* this is happening. What the heck is going on here? Drop every lingering belief long enough to ask yourself, "What if this whole thing is nothing more than a way to bring suffering to the life of a person who would not be suffering if this delusion didn't exist?"

See if you can stay with that sense of *"Do I know that?"* See if you can live for a while in the world of *"Is that true? How do I know that's true? Does anything other than the voices in my head support it?"*

Personal Survey on Voices

The questions in this survey are similar to those we worked with in regard to becoming aware of our conditioning. This exercise addresses the same experience from a slightly different angle. Again, to get a glimpse of unconsciously held beliefs and opinions, fill in the blanks with as many words and phrases as you can.

People should _____

I should _____

It's important to _____

God/my mother/father/partner/
children/friends want me to _____

A person who [is/has/does, etc.] _____

is _____

Our conditioning is reinforced through the voices that constantly repeat the messages. See if you can shift now from listening to the content of those messages to hearing what is communicated in ways other than through words.

- How would you describe the tone of the voices speaking to you?

- What is the quality of what is communicated by the voices?

- Do the voices sound friendly? Do they seem to like you?

- Is there anyone you speak to in the same way in which the voices speak to you?

- Are there particular themes that the voices speak about?

- Do you know anyone who uses the same type of speech as these voices? Who is that? How would you describe that type of speech?

- Can you list some of the names that the voices use in addressing you?

Remember: *You are looking for awareness in order to better see the ways in which you have been conditioned. Your conditioning is not who you are. Please do not allow conditioning to use your awareness against you.*

Seeing into the Issue by Attending to Self-Talk

Now it's time to attend closely to those voices that are talking to you about your issue.

What do I say to myself because I don't [work for myself]?

The illusion of control and the illusion of a separate self are neck-in-neck in the survival system race. Actually, they are not in competition, but are two aspects of the same competitor, supporting and spurring one another on to victory. Perhaps a better image is a tag team in wrestling. When the illusion of control gets weary (or ceases temporarily to be effective), the illusion of a separate self jumps in. Here is a description of how this works by someone who is looking at it closely.

JOANNA

I spend most of my time in three ways: (1) working on urgent things, meeting deadlines, and complaining; (2) numbing myself with junk food, alcohol, TV, and murder mysteries; or (3) lonely, depressed, and catatonic.

(1) When I finish a big project, after having complained throughout about the pressure, instead of feeling good about it and celebrating, I start looking around for the next emergency, the next urgent thing that must be accomplished that will help me avoid #2.

(2) When there are no more emergencies, or when I just can't work anymore, instead of relaxing for a while and being present to my life, I check out: time for junk food, alcohol, and mindless entertainment. I constantly mistake going numb and brain-dead for comfort and relaxation. Intellectually, I know they are not synonymous,

but it's a very old habit, and it gets me almost every day. Part of the motivation is that if I can check out fast enough, I don't have to face #3.

(3) When I (ego) decide to grab this problem by the horns and do something different—stay present in the evenings and not go numb, not be such a slug—an insidious conditioned loop kicks in that sounds something like this: First voice: "You are such a loser. Why don't you go out and do something fun? You can't think of anything fun? Then why don't you volunteer at the hospital? No? How about going to a bookstore? A bar? Taking a walk?" Second voice: "I'm bored with those things. They feel like lonely things to be doing. I have no imagination. If I were an imaginative person, and if I had any character at all, I wouldn't be stuck in this dead-end life." I feel (ego/a particular subpersonality feels) defeated, lonely, left out, hopeless, depressed, powerless, and (I suspect although I can't prove it) angry.

There are many ironies in all this. I have vowed to take refuge in Bodhi, Dharma, and Sangha. Instead, I take refuge in urgency, mindlessness, and depression. I have a life that most humans on this planet can only dream about, and a huge part of me is afraid of getting to the end of my life and feeling like I wasted it. Friends tell me I am funny, creative, and have a wonderful imagination. Self-hate can take all of the above and beat me bloody with them.

The bodily sensations involved in this conditioning are located in my back, near my waist, left side, over the kidney area. I just realized this today. It is intriguing. And I am afraid.

❋   ❋   ❋

My encouragement is to stay with finding the physical location of the emotions—slowly, patiently, just noticing where reactions are located. It is helpful to reach the very first sensation of a process of suffering and find that the sensation you are feeling has nothing to do with what your conditioning has turned it into. For example, I feel a twinge, a tiny movement in my solar plexus, and because I am not paying attention, the conditioning races off to an assumption that something is wrong, then the mind starts scanning. I'm projecting all over everyone, the stories are getting wilder, the fear is growing—oh, no! What is wrong?

When I find that little twinge, through just watching subtle movements in the body, I realize that the sensation is just a sensation. The only problem is my conditioned reaction to it and my tendency not to be present for the reaction. Eventually, I can feel that twinge and just recognize an old friend. It doesn't mean anything, and I don't need to do anything about it.

Locating where the emotion is centered in the body is very helpful in becoming aware of exactly what is going on—and it is the subject of the next chapter.

CHAPTER SEVEN

EMOTION:
Finding the Epicenter

The term I use for the main subpersonality that drove my early approach to life is "rageoholic," suggesting that my relationship to rage was much like that of an alcoholic's to alcohol. I would never have admitted that I could not live without rage—quite the opposite. I would have said that my violent temper was the worst of my traits and that I would love to be rid of it. But like alcohol for an alcoholic, fury was my ally, my solace, my comfort, my necessity. Explosive anger was the way I coped with a life that seemed intolerable to me.

I never knew why I was angry. I had no idea what anger was or how it worked. I can remember attending a "personal growth weekend" at the beginning of my attempts to gain some insight into myself and being dumbfounded when the facilitator asked us to feel our hearts beating. What?! Feel my heart beating? What the hell does that mean?! It made me furious! What a stupid notion! How can you feel your heart beat? I nearly got up and left right then. But for some part of me, feeling my heartbeat was an intriguing idea, and so, fortunately, I stayed.

During that period, I had several moments of "awakening" about the role of emotion in my life. The first occurred while I was building the cabin in Oregon. On long afternoons when I didn't want to do anything that involved sawing more boards or hammering more nails, I would get on my mini-motorcycle and head for the little town about ten miles up the road. Going into that town was like stepping into the last century (not the most recent last century, the one before that). Except for the scattering of battered pickup trucks and a neon sign or two, it could have been the Wild West of the 1870s or 1880s.

I always went to the general store, Ye Old Mercantile, which sold hardware, fabrics, groceries, liquor, and drugstore items. In the back was a huge potbellied wood stove surrounded by rocking chairs. In the afternoon, all the old duffers would gather around that stove, lean back in their rockers, and tell tall tales of the days of yore. I'd always loved hearing about "how it used to be." I had known since I was a kid that I belonged more in the previous century than in the one in which I found myself. Simplicity, quiet, no phones, no television, no knowing what everyone else is doing around the world—my kind of lifestyle. And these fellows had *lived* it!

One afternoon as I sat listening to my favorite old guy telling a story about his boyhood, I watched in horror as a familiar scene played out in my mind. I silently screamed, "Nooooo!" as I imagined myself doubling up my fist, drawing it back, and hitting my beloved old fellow in the face, knocking him backwards out of his rocker. I'm pretty sure that nothing registered on my face. I'd had years of practice hiding the kinds of violent thoughts and images that occupied my mind.

I continued to sit and listen for a while, but inside I felt sick. Even in this setting, with these kind old people, I was a monster—a violent, inhuman, depraved monster.

On my drive home, I experienced a flash of clarity, a split second of intuitive knowing that changed my life. What I saw in that infinitesimal gap in the conditioned self-image was that I didn't have that fantasy of hitting the old man because I was a monster or because I hated him or because of anything he did or said—*I had that reaction because I loved him!*

The "threat" was a feeling of affection that occurred on the sensation level, below my ability to perceive. I would feel the love (which I did not realize), and the next thing I knew, my fist would be pulling back. The sensation of love was followed by a burst of energy pushing the feeling away, which turned into pushing the "object" away, which turned into the violence of hitting. And the feeling I was having was not rage, but horror and revulsion at what I was doing.

As is true for many people, in my life up until then, love had meant pain. Loving people meant opening myself up to ridicule, humiliation, torture, and abuse. So, when I felt love for him, the conditioned survival that had enabled me to make it through living with my "loved ones" kicked in to protect me from feeling that extraordinarily dangerous emotion called love. For the first time in my life, I saw another view of myself, and I had sympathy for the person I saw.

I didn't realize it at the time, but in those few moments around the stove and on my drive home, I had experienced the terrible bondage of my social conditioning—and then the freedom of centered awareness. I had projected onto the old man my conditioned attitudes about simplicity and goodness. When threatened, even by love, I became a subpersonality who had the ability to keep at a distance anyone whose potential friendship might make me feel inclined to drop my defenses. In a disidentified moment, in the space between conditioned thoughts, there was an awareness of a larger reality, a clarity from which I could see how the whole process worked. I could see also that the way I had learned to view myself and others was limited and inaccurate.

That intuitive moment of clarity greatly intensified my interest in the awareness I was gaining from meditation.

Practicing with Emotions

What exactly is emotion? I readily confess to not knowing what emotion is. Of course if someone is sobbing or furious or frightened, I can recognize that behavior and attach the appropriate label. But what is emotion itself? When I examine how I experience emotion within myself, I can't find anything other than physical sensations with names attached to them.

When I observe myself, I see a movement of energy through various parts of the body. Some of the sensations that result from the movement of energy I have been conditioned to enjoy. The pleasant sensations come with labels such as happiness, ease, relaxation, joy, peace, bliss, comfort, affection, and love—"positive" emotions. Other sensations that result from the movement of energy are those that I am conditioned not to enjoy—anger, fear, hatred, resentment, irritation, sadness, jealousy, envy, which are considered "negative" emotions.

The following exercise will help you become more aware of exactly what you experience as emotion.

Find a comfortable position, close your eyes, and take two or three long, deep breaths. See if you can allow all of your attention to stay with the movement of the breath, and allow yourself to let go of any concerns or distractions.

Now, recall a time when you were feeling happy. Let yourself fully recall a particular time or situation, and put yourself into that scene. Then just take time to notice. Where in your body do you feel the happiness? What does it feel like?

Take another long, deep breath, and recall your most recent sadness. Again, take time to notice. Where in your body do you feel sadness? What does sadness feel like?

After taking another breath or two, repeat this process with fear. Where do you feel fear? What does it feel like?

Where do you feel love? What does love feel like in your body?

Where do you feel anger? What does anger feel like?

How about resentment?

Can you feel peace? Where do you feel peace?

What about joy? Where do you feel joy? How does joy feel?

During the rest of the day, observe closely where in your body you feel particular emotions. See if you can detect how you feel about the emotion. Is it acceptable to you, unacceptable to you, or are you indifferent to it?

As you are noticing emotion—what it is, where it is, and how you respond to it—consider this. Emotion makes things seem real. Many people hold an unexamined belief that emotion means something is true. That is not so, but the level of emotion, the presence or absence of emotion, often determines our relationship with a particular piece of life content.

Personal Survey on Emotion

* How do you know that someone is important to you?

* What would you think if a friend died and you felt nothing?

- What would you think if someone stole something from you and you had no reaction?

- Would you stay in a job if the thrill was gone? How about a romance or a marriage?

- How do you know when you really want something?

Remember: *You are seeking awareness to better see the ways in which you have been conditioned. Your conditioning is not who you are. Please do not allow conditioning to use your awareness against you.*

I came from a very emotional family, although I never thought of it that way since the only emotion we ever expressed was anger. We didn't seem emotional. We never talked about feelings; no one had any as far as I could tell. We just screamed, yelled, and threw things.

When I first began to explore the subject of emotion, it didn't take long to sense that I was carrying around a lot of unexpressed sadness. I was terrified by that discovery, but since emotion was so unacceptable to me, I didn't experience the terror as such; I just resisted. My response was, I don't want to think about that. When I finally did think about it—our family, my horrible relationship with my father, the loss of my mother, my attempted suicide, the breakup of my marriage, everything I had put and was putting my daughter through—I thought, *I can't cry. If I ever start, I'll never stop.* I could picture myself crying to death.

Cry I did, and die I did not. I subsequently read about some research described by Elisabeth Kübler-Ross showing that a "true" emotion lasts only a matter of seconds. If we allow ourselves to actually feel what we are feeling, the sensations pass through the body very quickly. The reason a particular emotion lingers is that we first resist it and then we cling to it. Because of the *meaning* we have attached to a particular set of sensations/energy, we believe that feeling a particular emotion says something about us—that feeling a particular way means we have to do something or stop doing something. Not wanting to go through all the *meaning* involved, we try to avoid, suppress, or deny the emotion. Then when we finally succumb to the experience, it says so much about who we are and how life is that we cling to it, not wanting to let go of the identity.

Once again, children can be our role models. With children, none of it means anything; it is entirely straightforward. One child takes a toy away from the other. The toyless child wails piteously. The toyless child recovers, bops the thief over the head, retrieves the toy, and returns to a sunny disposition, while the now toyless child wails piteously. An adult walks in with cookies and milk, and the children drop their tears and toys and clamor for goodies. The message for us is, when something hurts, wail about it. When the hurt is gone, move on to the next thing.

Because this process is so involved—and because it is crucial to see through it—let's go back through it using examples.

HOLDING ON

Bernadette is in a long-term, committed, monogamous relationship. She finds herself with a crush on Coleman. She feels a set of sensations that she has always known are somehow wrong. She hides the crush from everyone, including herself. What these sensations say about her is that she is scandalous, bad, wrong. When she is finally forced to acknowledge to herself and to her partner what she has been feeling, she is embarrassed, humiliated, and guilty. This is living proof that she always has been a bad person and continues to be a bad person.

❊   ❊   ❊

Colleen has a wonderful new friend. Amy is open, friendly, fun, generous, bright, and talented. As time passes, however, and Colleen gets to know Amy better, she finds that Amy has other attributes that Colleen finds less admirable. Amy is emotionally dramatic, demanding, and controlling. It is not acceptable to Colleen to be judgmental of her friend, so she makes excuses for Amy's behavior or takes responsibility for any upsets or misunderstandings. Finally, the proverbial straw that breaks the camel's back: Amy borrows Colleen's car in an emergency and brings it back filthy and out of gas. Colleen's level of anger and resentment shocks her. She sees that once again she has been overly generous, gullible, and left holding the bag. She's not sure whom she hates more, Amy or herself. She has been through this so many times—will she never learn?

❊   ❊   ❊

The difference between children and adults is that the children just respond to what is there; it's completely clean. By the time we're conditioned, however, we drag in so much meaning. It *means* something about Bernadette that she has a crush on Coleman. It *means* something about Colleen that her relationship with Amy is not as she would have wished. The whole thing is just a setup to reinforce the conditioned beliefs about ourselves.

We have so many bizarre messages about emotion. It's okay to feel a certain way under one set of circumstances, but not feel another way, ever. If you are male, certain emotions are available to you. If you are female, other emotions are available to you. You may feel this way up to this age, but not after. You should feel these feelings, but only in the presence of these people, or better yet, only when you're alone. You should be sensitive and care deeply, but not show what you feel.

Working with the Epicenter

The epicenter in an earthquake is the point where the movement originates. We can find an "epicenter" in the body that is the locus of sensations that are associated with emotions. The purpose of the following exercise is to get to know our emotions in the place where they arise and are experienced most intensely.

I will ask you to repeat this exercise several times, so read through the whole progression until it is clear in your mind. Then set the instructions aside and proceed.

Sit down, get comfortable, and turn your attention to your breath. Take ten natural, relaxed breaths.

Just notice what's going on with you. Notice where your attention goes, and then gently bring it back to the breath. If you feel tension in your body, breathe into the tension, and as you exhale, let the tension leave your body with the exhalation. Feel your body let go into whatever is supporting it—a chair, a cushion, or the floor. No tightness or tension is required to hold your body in place.

When you feel as relaxed and present as you can for right now, turn your attention to the issue you are working on. Let yourself be open to the issue and its effects on you, until you can feel yourself responding to it in your body and in your emotions.

As you continue to go over the issue, notice how your body reacts. If you're aware of an emotional component, notice the form it takes.

Allow sensations to build, and see if you can find their epicenter, the focal point where they originate. Become aware of exactly where emotion resides in your body, where the epicenter is.

Now, turn all of your attention back to your breath. Feel the breath as it enters your body. Feel the body expand with the incoming breath and contract with the exhalation. Feel your body slow down as it relaxes with the exhalation. Feel it letting go, keeping your focus on the breath. Each exhalation brings you more ease and comfort.

Let go of everything other than being right here, focused on the breath, feeling the breath in the body. When your body feels relaxed and comfortable, look to see what has happened to the issue.

Now, turn your attention back to the issue. Repeat this sequence several times until you are able to watch the issue come into existence and allow it to disappear. Each time you bring it into existence, look to see where it is experienced in your body.

See if you can turn your attention to that place in your body that is the epicenter of the issue, and feel the existence of the issue without needing to tell yourself any of the stories.

Here are some reports of people's experience with this exercise:

RAY

I was able to locate my issue in my chest mostly, a little in my arms. It was a sensation I've sometimes identified as longing. When I returned all of my attention back to the breath, the sensation dissipated. What I want to mention is that when I bring my attention to my chest without first telling myself the story of my issue, there is no sensation I can identify as longing. This brought up a sense of fear.

I found myself wondering what this means. Does it mean that the issue isn't real? What will happen to me if I don't have the issue? Isn't it necessary that I maintain such issues so I can go forward in life? (My issue is about things I haven't been able to bring myself to do.) I find it amazing that I would fear giving up these thoughts that have only served to keep me unhappy rather than help me accomplish things I think I want to do. I hope the fear doesn't keep me from continuing with this work.

SANDY

As I was sitting with my "problem" (feeling like I'm too emotionally attached to my mother), this is what I noticed.

At first the epicenter was around my right ear with words and images of my mother yelling at me and criticizing me as a small child. The physical sensations and images were those of being slapped on the face. I tried to just feel the motion from right cheek to left without staying involved in the pictures and words.

The words and images quickly changed but were still about my mother. The epicenter moved to my heart area, and I felt contracted and cold. I saw myself as a little girl cringing, afraid of her. The images and sensations changed again. I felt sensations in my lower back and buttocks area, along with images of being hit with a fly-swatter as a child. I tried to disidentify from the images and sounds and just get into the sensations. All this happened in fairly rapid succession. I also felt angry, with sensations in my forehead and my whole body.

When the sensations went to the heart area, I realized that it's not that I'm too emotionally attached to my mother, but that I've been afraid of her, afraid to feel my true emotions. I wasn't trying to figure this out intellectually, more like it came to me. It was a freeing insight. I continued to feel the wave-like motion going partway up and down my lower spine until I was primarily feeling the waves and not involved in the drama of images and words.

The whole thing went away. I haven't worried or been concerned with it since. Images and voices still come up, but I don't take them as personally and they don't last as long. I used to think I had to be "loyal" to the frightened image of me as a child and maintain—hold on to—that image, but now I realize that my loyalty is to the person I am now and my present health.

This certainly throws suspicion on all the other things I've considered a problem, because that issue has been bugging me for many years, and I've thought it was such a big thing that would require an enormous amount of work. I found out it wasn't even true! It's like a setup. I could work on it for years, but it would never go away because it wasn't there in the first place.

Things are usually not as they seem (I would go so far as to say that things are never as they seem) when viewed from ego-centricity. We stay stuck because, as the old saying goes, we're trying to fix things that aren't broken. We stay in a feeling-bad loop because we're afraid to examine what's going on, or we don't know that there's anything to examine. Until it occurs to us that what we have been taught to believe might not be the absolute truth, there is no reason to look for another reality.

When we realize or even have a healthy suspicion that other possibilities exist, often what keeps us from starting the exploration is the fear generated by egocentric conditioning fighting for survival. The voices will tell us that it will be too hard, too scary, and we'll see awful things about ourselves. But the result of the exploration is quite the opposite:

ERIN

When I did the exercise, much to my surprise I discovered something! I don't usually pay very close attention to what's going on in my body unless it's pain, and then I want it to just go away. So I didn't expect to see or feel anything with this exercise. My issue is irritation, my not-so-subtle form of anger, which appears when I'm mad at someone but unable to tell them I'm angry. It's my passive-aggressive way of letting folks know I'm angry without being angry (because the voices tell me anger is wrong). Anyway, as I brought up the feeling of irritation and paid attention to what was arising, my heart started hurting, and the pain extended up to my throat—a feeling very similar to that of holding back tears. There was an underlying feeling of sadness, like my heart hurt when I was angry or irritated. In my head, I know others hurt when I'm irritated at them. I want others to tell me when they're angry at me, yet I seem unable to do that myself, and so my irritation seems like a dishonest emotion. It feels like heartache—for them because of my passive-aggressiveness, and for me, because I beat myself up for not being able to be honest.

The beauty of this exercise is that I know the feelings are heart-centered, and it feels that because of that, there is compassion for the process. It feels like a loving sadness, kind of like grief, but for myself. I know that this is the way I do it at the present time, but the heart pain tells me that even though I'm hurting myself by reacting to things this way, love for myself is still there. This may not make any sense to anyone else, but thank goodness it does to me.

Seeing into the Issue by Observing Emotions

Now it's time to consider your issue in terms of your emotional response to it.

How do I feel about myself when I don't [work for myself]?

Once again, in this dualistic reality, I can feel two extremes and all the subtleties in between. I feel bad that I'm not doing what I want to do. I feel frustrated and a little scared, because I really want to do this and I can't. Where does that leave me? Feeling out of control, feeling angry, and feeling ripped off. I'm a good person—why can't I have this simple thing I want? At the same time, though, I feel right: See, nothing ever works for me. I never get what I want. I knew it would turn out like this.

In both cases, I feel separate and in control. I am me and I am the star, the author, of my life. I am me, and I *know.*

Here are some additional questions for your consideration:

- How do you feel about having the issue that you chose to work with?

- How do you feel when the issue isn't present? When the issue begins to arise? When you are in the middle of the issue? When it's over and you have failed again?

- Which emotions are involved?

- Explore each emotion in turn. Can you hear the judgments that accompany each one?

- Where in your body do you feel these emotions?

- What does it say about you that you are a person who has these feelings?

- Do you know which feelings stop you from being different in relation to this issue?

MARTHA

I have been working on finding the epicenter of my issue, although as you warned, my issue does tend to change itself from time to time. So, I started out with the problem that my husband finds so much fault with me— and I find fault with him. The faults tend to cover many domains: parenting, work, and home. I tried finding out where the problem was in my body, and it turned out to be where I breathe. I could get relaxed and be fine, then when I imagined one of our exchanges, I would have dif-

ficulty breathing. My breathing would be shallow, I wanted to cough, I couldn't get air. The problem is close to and right below my throat. This makes sense because this actually has been the pattern for several years. When I was having a particularly difficult time a couple of years ago related to this issue, what happened was that I felt I couldn't breathe, and I coughed instead.

So I've been trying to do as you suggested—getting relaxed and then thinking of the problem, seeing what my body does, and trying to breathe through it. Sometimes it works. I can feel my body conjuring up sensations out of whole cloth and wrapping my feelings and thoughts in this sensation of being strangled. I breathe into it, and it subsides and goes away. I've had some success in seeing through it, in breathing through it, but not always. It seems that sometimes the sensation comes up on its own, or sometimes the sensation is so uncomfortable it's just very hard to breathe through it.

I've been trying to evoke my problem, breathe through it, even knowing that it is "my" problem. Sometimes I get the sensation of ego wanting me to suffer. All of a sudden, lots of "problems" will arise, not just the one I chose to focus on. It's as if the goal is to make me feel alone and isolated, but "real." Then sometimes I can watch the problems subside, and I know they aren't real. I try to remember that I'm not the problems, not separate, just part of the flow. When the problems subside, it's a little like having my vision clear for a moment, and I see where I'm walking or standing, and it's an interesting glimpse of how our thoughts capture us and take us away.

It's important to notice how unhappy we make ourselves when people and the world do not operate in the way our beliefs say they should. And it's beneficial to be aware of how unhappy we make ourselves when we don't operate in the way our conditioning says we should. It can be very helpful to turn some of our attention away from endlessly focusing on what is going on "out there" toward examining the process of projection—the way we see aspects of ourselves as existing not within us but in others. The following chapter addresses how we are "captured and taken away" from ourselves, in Martha's words, by projecting our own concerns onto the external world.

CHAPTER EIGHT

PROJECTION:
How Are You/How Am I?

To me, the single most powerful tool available to us in our attempt to go beyond our egocentric social conditioning and move into conscious, compassionate awareness is recognizing our projections. Projection means attributing one's own traits to others. From the perspective of spiritual practice, everything you experience is your projection. Everything you think, feel, see, and know is a mirror of yourself. You look out at the world, and because you are looking from yourself through the filter of your personality, the only thing to see is you. You think it's the world you're seeing, but it is the totality of your own preferences, habits, beliefs, and assumptions projected onto the world. The fact that we are unconscious of this does not mean it is not so.

When I was allowed to enter the silent monastery where I trained, I knew I had arrived. Here was a holy place filled with holy people. I would walk through those gates, leaving all my "baggage" outside, as required by tradition, and I, too, would become a holy person. Within six weeks, however, I had completely recreated the world I had intended to leave behind, from childhood to my last miserable relationship. In the monastery, one person became my father, another my brother—in spite of the fact that I had never exchanged a word with anyone there.

I needed bodies to people my world, to play the familiar roles in the drama of ensuring my survival, and these were the only folks available.

As you can probably imagine, it didn't take long for me to decide that I had made a big mistake. With all those projections, the monastery was transformed—it was clearly not a holy place, and the others there were far from holy people. I stayed *in spite of them* (one more thing to file under "Blessings abound") and went on to have many more lessons in projection.

Some of my favorite lessons involved times when my teacher would go into one of his two primary modes, senile and cranky. When he showed signs of senility, I got nervous. I had given up a perfectly good life (a believable description only from a great distance) to come to this godforsaken place and follow the direction of a guy who repeated the same things over and over and didn't make sense. When he was cranky, I got annoyed. *We're here to let go our egocentric conditioning,* I would think, *and he goes around acting like an irritable child.* He doesn't like this, he doesn't like that. Picky, picky, picky. Why doesn't he just grow up?

I'm almost too embarrassed to admit how long it took me to understand that *I* was the irritable child, projecting my own ego-centric conditioning onto him. I would be lost in my own conditioning, and he would seem so difficult. Then something would shift, I would move out of that particular identity, and suddenly he would appear to be in a completely different mood. I would be amazed. Or he would seem pretty reasonable, then something would happen that threatened some part of me, a defensive sub-personality would take over, and he looked like a madman. Again and again, we went through that. I don't know how he put up with it for so long. Well, actually I do. He knew I didn't know what I was doing. But still, I admire his restraint.

How Projection Works

The expressions "A person with a hammer sees nails every-where" and "A pickpocket sees only pockets" offer a glimpse into how projection works. Let's say I grew up conditioned to believe that "people get what they deserve." When I look out at the world, I am looking through the eyes of the part of me who believes that people get what they deserve. Therefore, what I see when I look out at the world is people getting what they deserve. If someone is doing well, it's because they deserve it. If someone is floun-dering, it's because they deserve it. I don't know how or why. I never even wonder about it. I just know that people are having the lives they deserve. When something goes my way, I feel good, knowing that I deserve good things: I work hard, and I'm fair and honest, so life should reward me. When something goes against me, I feel bad knowing that good things are being withheld from me, and I have an explanation for that, too: Sometimes I'm a lit-tle selfish and self-centered, and I need to be kept in line.

Is any of this true? No. But holding that belief system, oper-ating from an aspect of the personality who sees the world as a you-get-what-you-deserve-in-life proposition, I never see any-thing that fails to conform to my reality. A color-blind person sees the colors he sees and does not know what colors other people are seeing. Of course, we fail to notice one crucial fact: *We don't know that anyone is seeing exactly the same color another per-son is seeing.*

I love a particular color, I think it is the height of good taste, I feel marvelous when I'm near it, and I want to paint the whole house that color. You think it is an appalling color, and my even considering painting the house with it makes you question my sanity. Are we experiencing the same color?

As stated earlier, human beings have the built-in ability to experience themselves as separate. As soon as that ability is developed, "I" is I and "you" are you. "I" is the subject, "you" are the object. "It" and "they" are also objects. In fact, everything that exists is an object to my subject. "I" is the center of everything. "I" is the right, the correct, and, truth be told, the *only* perspective.

Great suffering results from the ability of "I" to see everyone and everything as object—but that suffering is nothing compared to the suffering that results from "I" seeing "me" as an object. The "I" who knows and is right, the "I" who is conditioned to accept a particular perspective, sees "me," the one who is not conforming to its standards, as other, as a threat to its survival. "I" decides "me" is overweight and puts "me" on a diet. "I" watches, monitors, judges, criticizes, rewards, sabotages, and generally makes "me" miserable in the process. I-as-subject projects its standards and values onto me-as-object and sets about making me be the right way.

I compare the relationship between I-subject and me-object with that between master and slave. Each egocentric illusion of a separate self has one person to control, drive, punish, direct, beat, humiliate, and nag: one's self.

Some people have the I-master, you-slave relationship with others—partner, children, employees, or subordinates—and we can hear it in their language when they address these people. Most of us, though, have that relationship primarily within ourselves, and we can learn to hear that as well. The projections of the I-master onto the me-slave are right there in the internal voices, the self-talk. "You idiot! Why did you do that? What's the matter with you? Can't you do anything right?" Periodically, we hear from the me-slave: "What's wrong with me? Why can't I ever do anything right? I'm never going to learn. I'm just hopeless."

At what point does I-subject feel its isolation as a threat rather than a support to its survival? Egocentricity has an amazing ability to hunker down and cling to its separate identity regardless of the threat. Externals may come and go— possessions can go, friends can go, family can go, health can go, the good opinion of others can go—but "I" endures. The I-subject may need to alter its view of its surroundings, but the game plan remains the same: *I will survive.*

We recognize this phenomenon in medical science. What constitutes the I-subject? Is it the leg? No, the legs can go and "I" will be all right. Is it the arm? No, I can live without my arms. How about emotions? No, actually, emotions can be threatening, and I can live without them. I can even live without perception—without sight or hearing or smell or taste or sensation. Finally, we see an I-subject clinging to its survival in spite of having lost everything.

Where Is the "I"?

What is this I-subject? It is certainly worthwhile to question its dominion over one's life. I encourage you to explore this carefully because the root cause of suffering is this illusion of separation and our devotion to enabling this illusion to control our lives.

This assumption of "I" as separate from everything else is so fundamental to human perception that it is almost impossible to glimpse, let alone grasp. This is the phenomenon we talk about as "skin"; seeing through the assumption would be like seeing one's own skin from the inside out. "But I'm me!" the illusion protests. "I am real! I can see, hear, feel, think—of course I'm real." Agreed: but a real illusion. Again, the reason we cannot grasp this is that the illusion is trying to see the illusion. The illusion has already decided that it *is* reality and everything else is illusion. The point is whether or not the self is separate, not whether or not the illusion is maintained through the illusion that experience has an experiencer.

In his book *On Having No Head*, Douglas Harding pointed out that our actual experience of life is of being a stalk, the body, which ends at the chest and shoulders, upon which sits the entire universe. We can't directly experience ourselves as having a head; we simply assume we are looking out through the eyes in our head because we see others doing that, and when we look in the mirror, that's what we see. But our *experience* is of an undifferentiated world of colors, shapes, textures, sounds, feelings, and sensations, all existing in one reality, roughly in the spot where we think of our head as being. All that exists, exists on top of the stalk that I call me.

The truly amazing next step in this realization is that the stalk I call me is included in the total existence that extends outward from the top of the stalk. My actual *experience* is that *nothing is separate*. I cannot say that any one thing is separate from any other one thing because they all occupy the same space—the space that exists, and contains, the stalk that I call me.

We have no evidence that there is anything outside of ourselves. We cannot prove that there is. Lao Tzu observed that it was impossible to know if he was a man dreaming he is a butterfly or a butterfly dreaming he is a man. The egocentric illusion of separation called "I" can become impatient with this sort of nonsense. "I know what I am. I know I am not a dreaming butterfly!" Really? The assertion itself proves the opposite. The illusion *believes* itself to be real; we do not *know*.

Egocentricity lives in its own conditioned reality, projects that reality out, and sees that reality confirmed. Here's an example:

A STUDY IN CONTRASTS

Frank grew up in Southern California. His father is a lawyer, and his mother is a pediatrician. Money was never an issue, the sky was always clear, and life was a romp in the sun. Frank's was a liberal, affluent circle, and even when he realized, and announced, that he was gay, there was barely a ripple in the easy simplicity of his life.

Juan was raised in a poor neighborhood in Chicago, the oldest son of a Mexican restaurant worker. Juan's mother cleaned houses for families in the wealthier neighborhoods across town, and Juan had accompanied her until he was old enough to go to school. Life was always a struggle, and Juan learned from an early age to be careful, work hard, and stay invisible. When he realized he was gay, Juan began to save the money he would need to move to California—he knew he could never let his family know about his homosexuality.

Opposites certainly can attract, and Juan and Frank were attracted to one another. As with many relationships, at first their differences went unnoticed, or were a source of interest and delight, but soon their beliefs and assumptions began to take precedence over their affection. Frank projected that Juan was closed and secretive. Juan projected that Frank was frivolous and insincere.

Was either right? No. Frank interpreted Juan's actions through his own conditioning. He looked out through his sunny, relaxed experience of life and saw Juan's reserved caution as secretive and closed. Juan looked out through his careful, quiet struggling and saw Frank's ease in dealing with life as superficial and shallow.

❋　❋　❋

We all do this constantly. If I am wearing a pair of glasses with red lenses and you have on glasses with blue lenses, we will not be able to agree on what color things are. Even if someone told us both that the walls are white and the floor is gray, you would see them as a shade of blue, and I as a shade of red.

So, what are Frank, Juan, and the rest of us to do? We can each realize that we are projecting from our own small viewpoint and that we actually have no idea what anyone (often including ourselves) is doing. The best that Frank, Juan, and the rest of us can do is acknowledge that we: (1) don't know what is true for the other; (2) are operating from our own biases; and (3) sincerely want to know what things look like from the other's point of view. That is, Juan might say to Frank, "If I were concerned about someone being secretive and closed, I would be coming from an experience of needing to hide certain things to feel safe, and I would probably feel sympathetic. I can sense that your concern arises from a different experience, and because I care about our relationship, I would like to know what is going on with you. Would you be willing to tell me about that?"

How kind that would be, how conducive to understanding and peace. But we aren't conditioned that way. We have been taught to believe that our own view of the world is right and true, and it is essential to our survival that we be right in our particular assessment of life. Is that true? No, but we have been taught to believe it is. We have all the information we need to understand that other people don't experience life as we do, yet because we have been conditioned to believe that there is only one right answer, our only conclusion can be that the other is wrong.

When it comes to seeing the magnitude of projection, many people stumble over the fact that other people agree with their projections. "I checked with everyone who knows him, and they all agree that Bob is a jerk. It can't be projection if we all see the same thing." Most emphatically it can. How? We tend to live our lives with people who share the same social conditioning we have. If you notice, people tend to travel in packs, and the packs tend to be homogeneous. When we go behind superficial differences, we see the similarities that draw and keep people together. What matters much less than being the same color, religion, economic level, age, and background is that *we hold the same opinions.*

Are there moments of clarity that are without projection? Yes, but "you"—or more accurately "I"—won't be having them. Clarity is when "I" is not in charge.

Owning Our Projections

As you can probably imagine, over the years, people have challenged me about the statement that there is no objective reality because everything we experience is our projection. "Well, but what about . . . ," and "Yes, but isn't it possible that . . . ?" Here is the point: I am not looking for loopholes. I am attempting to see through and let go the egocentric programming that is causing my suffering and robbing me of the full life that is my birthright. If there were moments of clarity in which I perceived an objective reality, what would I have gained? I ask you to think about that carefully. If I could prove that, in truth, Bob *really is* a jerk, what would I have? Egocentricity would be "right," and I would be—where?

Here, though, is why that will never happen. Let's say that you have a moment of crystal- clear perception, transcending the illusion of a separate self, with no projection of yourself onto the world. By the time you register that, the clarity is gone and you are projecting again. Your choice of words, the framework in which you place the experience, the way you position yourself in relationship to it, are all projections of the conditioning that maintains the illusion of what you think of as you.

In the on-line workshops I offer, in which people's e-mailed responses to questions are posted for all the participants to see, I received this communication:

STACY

Help! I am feeling left out and unique. My response to the "what is a friend?" question was left out of the class, perhaps understandably because my answers did not fit in to the point you were trying to make. Yet I have thought about this, and I feel profoundly sad because my concept of a friend is not unconditional love and acceptance. Rather, I feel I confront those I truly love and care for. I don't accept any and all behavior from them. And I feel most loved by those who will confront me (in a loving way). I think this is the exact opposite of what most people feel. And your suggestion that our voices are not being friend-like because they don't fit the definition of unconditional love and acceptance doesn't work for me. To me, a friend would confront me.

My question is, am I wrong to value honesty too highly? Am I wrong to confront others I love and hope they will confront me on my character defects? Most people don't operate like I do, but it feels right to me. I just told my mom the other day that I share really hard stuff with her because I want intimacy with her. I want to feel closer (I've never felt close to anyone that I can remember, I've always protected myself). I think my mom hates it when I'm honest with her, but our relationship is more real now than it has ever been, and I am starting to really feel.

❀   ❀   ❀

Let's explore what honesty is. What is it, and who defines what is honest? A few decades back, some segments of our society were afflicted with an epidemic of terrible honesty. "I have to be honest with you, I think that is the ugliest outfit I've ever seen." "Honestly, everyone agrees that you are too loud." I would like to offer a different approach to honesty—the honesty of owning one's projections.

While we may come into this life with certain predisposi-
tions, we don't come in with the standards, beliefs, assumptions,
philosophies, and opinions that society programs us with. Those
have to be imposed: Life is this way, you need to do that, that's
okay but that isn't, those are pretty, that's desirable, good people
should . . . you have to . . . you can't . . . . Those are belief systems, not truths.

Once we have completed the process of learning to "think for
ourselves"—that is, rearranging conditioned beliefs to suit our
own individual survival systems—we settle into believing that
we're right about what we experience. For instance, I know that
there is a right way and a wrong way to treat children. I know
who treats children well and who doesn't. I know what people's
behaviors mean about who they are. I know how people should
be treated based on whether they are behaving correctly or incor-
rectly, and I am qualified to let people know when they
are wrong.

In the socially conditioned world of suffering, all that is true.
People have been killing each other for as long as there have been
people because of exactly that: "I am right, and my survival is
paramount!"

However, in practicing awareness as part of a process of liberation, there is no way to be "right" and at the same time be free.
That is, as long as we are maintaining the world dictated by our
conditioning, we are stuck in suffering. Once we cease to maintain that world, we are free to be and do as we choose. Therefore,
as one who chooses not to be stuck, it behooves me to see through
this illusory maze of conditioning as quickly as possible. How
might I do that? *By owning my own projections.*

Each of us projects from an opinion that we have learned, an
opinion that not everyone holds, and that, in fact, is not "true"
anywhere but in our own programmed heads. So, now someone
is going to be "honest" and "confront" others. I have no objection
to that, coming from the there-is-no-reason-to-do-or-not-to-do-

anything school of awareness practice. But I wish that anyone taking this confrontational approach would first answer the questions below. (Please consult something other than your conditioning to find answers.)

- Why would I want to confront someone about their faults?

- Who would be helped by such a confrontation? Who would feel better as a result of it?

- How do I know I'm right?

- Do I feel any urgency about this? (Urgency, along with fear and a sense of deprivation, loss, and something being wrong, is a signal that we are operating out of an illusion of a separate self that is attempting to control life and protect itself.)

- Do I have unresolved issues about the subject in question?

- Have I been invited to confront this person, or would it be intrusive?

The Unacceptable

What we find difficult or unacceptable "out there" is nothing more than a projection outward of what we have been taught to find unacceptable in ourselves. The spiritual teacher Gurdjieff had a student in his community who was intensely disliked by all the other students. One day, the student decided he'd had enough of being disliked, and he left. When Gurdjieff learned what had happened, he ran after the student, caught up with him—and paid him to return. His reasoning was that without the student there, the rest of the community would find it easier to hide from themselves the qualities they despised but undeniably possessed, qualities projected onto the despised student.

We want to rid ourselves of that annoying, cantankerous, obstinate, foolish, selfish, overbearing, egocentric, manipulative, lazy, arrogant, stupid individual because when that person is gone, we don't have to be aware of those parts of ourselves. "I am not an aggressive person," we may say, "until I get around him." Or, "I am a patient person, until I'm around her." "I am generous myself, and I can't stand users and takers." All projection.

This is why, as we develop, we are constantly splitting into various identities. With enough fragmentation, I can be one person when I am alone or with my selected circle; and another, opposite, person when I am with those who mirror the aspects of myself I have been conditioned to hate and reject, and not see any inconsistency in myself. I am the way I am, the way that fits with my self-image, the way that is acceptable to the people on whom my survival depends, and those other behaviors and feelings and thoughts are not me. Those are anomalies. In fact, they don't really exist—that was just an accident that happened because of what someone else was doing. That person, that situation, *forced* me to temporarily become someone I'm not.

We have a whole language for this phenomenon: *I wasn't myself. That's not like me. Something just came over me.* These are all ways of explaining away, of denying, that we are more than the limited package that society demands and that we agree to pretend to be. The ways we are that are unacceptable we simply project "out there" on to "them"—and whole cultures collude in such scapegoating.

I would suggest that the problems that plague our nation have the same cause as the problems that plague and have plagued *all* nations. It is not that some people do not live up to the standards of other people and must be changed or gotten rid of. It is that being conditioned to live in a state of ignorance and delusion, we despise ourselves for not being as we should be, and we project our self-hatred outward on to the "others" whom we blame for our own lack of awareness and responsibility.

It is my prediction that as people realize what projection is and how it works, there will be less labeling of people (as in diagnoses of mental illness and emotional problems); fewer suspicions of immorality; fewer generalizations about minorities, religious groups, and homosexuals; and fewer claims about women's emotional nature. As soon as we learn to trace comments back to the mouth and mind of the speaker, rather than automatically following the pointing finger, we will be a quieter, more aware society.

Personal Survey on Projection

Here are several ways to explore projection in yourself:

Think of three words you would use to describe traits in someone you dislike or do not admire. If you want to have the full experience, write the words down.

"_____ is _____,
_____, and _____."

Consider for a moment that those are words that you have chosen, out of all the words available, to describe this person. Do you think that person would use those words to describe themselves? Would everyone else use those words? Can you imagine a friend of this person using those descriptive words? These are the words you have chosen.

Now write, "My experience of _____ is
_____, _____, and _____."
Notice if that feels more accurate. This is not a universal
truth; it is your own experience of this person.

Now try this: "It is my projection that _____
is _____, _____, and
_____." Notice how that feels.

And here is the big one: "I am _____,
_____, and _____." These are
the same three words to describe you that you used to
describe the other person. You cannot know these things
about someone else if you don't know them in yourself.

"But I'm not like that," I can hear someone screaming. "I'd
never be that way." Not possible. The trait or characteristic that
person exhibits may not be a dominant trait or characteristic in
you, but the standard for it resides within you or you would not
have chosen that description. Here are a couple of responses I
received from people who did this exercise.

ROSS

*It's true! The person who bugs me the most is a
reflection of the qualities in myself that I do not like. The
person I chose is undisciplined, disorganized, and does
sloppy work. I have a side (maybe even a whole personality!) like this, and I don't like it. If I hate this other person, I can distance myself. It gets into what I was taught:
lazy is bad, disorganized is bad. That part of me is bad,
so stuff it down.*

MONA

The universe is telling me something, since I just read a statement by Stephen Covey in which he says about feedback: "Ask yourself, 'Will this feedback be helpful, or does it just fulfill my own need to set this person straight?'" I do see that some of the things I detest about my friend are the same things I detest in myself.

❋   ❋   ❋

Remember our look at postures? Each opinion, idea, belief, and assumption we hold is a conditioned response to something we have encountered in life. Many of these contain a *should* element.

I believe that people who don't work are lazy, so I should work to avoid laziness.

People who show affection in public seem low class, so I shouldn't act that way since I don't want people to think I'm low class.

I believe that wearing out-of-fashion clothes is a serious breach of common sense as well as good taste.

I wear clothes from the used clothing store because I want to make the clear statement that our rampant consumerism has got to stop.

It is more difficult to sense the implied *should* when we are operating from the opposite side of the continuum on an issue. For example, if my family places a lot of value on saving money,

I may go to the opposite extreme so as to appear as different from them as possible. We can see the *should* in the family's saving; it is more difficult to see the *should* in my not saving. With a little closer look, however, it is possible to see that the family and I are each equally trapped in our *shoulds* about the very same issue. And it's quite possible that if the family decided they'd saved enough and started a big spending campaign, I just might open a savings account.

The ways in which we can know that *should* is in there, even when it feels as if we are making a conscious choice, are that: (1) our behavior doesn't vary; (2) we would feel guilty if we did something different; and (3) we project people are judging us for the things we judge ourselves for.

Again, *we project that people are judging us for the very things we judge ourselves for.* People are judging us all the time. That's what we do as conditioned people—we judge. We have to judge because that's the only way we can know how we're doing in the process we have learned as the only way to ensure our survival. We compare ourselves to others as a way of determining our success rate. Here is the irony: We pay no attention to all the judgments that people make about us *as long as those judgments are in areas we have not been conditioned to care about.* We are obsessed with how we are being judged in our areas of concern, but actually have no idea what other people think because we are busy *projecting our judgments of ourselves onto them.*

Here's another projection exercise. Listen to your own self-talk about someone or something else, and change every "he," "she," and "they" to "I." If we each use our increased awareness to own our projections, we'll be taking huge steps toward ending the cruelty and suffering inherent in unconscious interactions.

Another exercise: Think of something—a person, an object, or an event—that you are drawn to for whatever reason. It does not need to be something you like; you could find yourself (or more precisely, your attention) drawn to something because you find it unsettling or unpleasant. When you decide what you want to focus on, write a paragraph or so on how you experience this individual or object or circumstance. Do the writing before you read on. Here is what I wrote for this exercise:

> My new antique secretary is beautiful in the way only that which is old and worn from love and appreciation can be beautiful. The wood was not expensive when new, but years of use have made it smooth and buttery. The decades of daily handling have also provided scrapes and scars, but somehow they only add to its character. It is a wonderful size and shape, not delicate, but sturdy and functional. One of my favorite things about this particular secretary, as compared to others I've seen, is that every inch of it is useable. There is nothing about it that is frilly or done just for show—it is made to work hard and work well. It has wide, deep storage areas, as well as lots of little nooks and crannies for thises and thats (and even secret places that only I know about), and a surface for writing personal things that is only available when the desk is open and can be left closed to conceal all those cubbies and treasure compartments when it's not in use. It used to have a lock and key, but the lock is broken and the key is long gone.

❊ ❊ ❊

Now, go through what you have written and mark through the nouns and pronouns that refer to what you're writing about, and insert "I" or "me" or "mine" in those places. Then read the revision. (It's actually helpful to read it aloud.) Here is mine:

> I am beautiful in the way only that which is old and worn from love and appreciation can be beautiful. I was not expen-

sive when new, but years of use have made me smooth and buttery. The decades of daily handling have also provided scrapes and scars, but somehow they only add to my character. Mine is a wonderful size and shape, not delicate, but sturdy and functional. One of my favorite things about me, as compared to others I've seen, is that every inch of me is useable. There is nothing about me that is frilly or done just for show—I am made to work hard and work well. I have wide, deep storage areas (!), as well as lots of little nooks and crannies for thises and thats (even secret places that only I know about), and a surface for writing personal things that is only available when I am open and can be left closed to conceal all those cubbies and treasure compartments when I'm not in use. I used to have a lock and key, but the lock is broken and the key is long gone.

❊　❊　❊

No wonder I love that secretary—it's me! Although I'm more comfortable thinking about the wide, deep storage areas in the secretary than in my body, I can say *yes* to every word and every sentence.

With this awareness, we can have great sympathy for the person whose car is stolen, whose house is broken into, or whose child is kicked out of school for abusing drugs. Imagine the level of projection of oneself into those "externals." We see two people in a fight over a "fender-bender" and might wonder what the fuss is about, until we consider that those people are not fighting over cars; they are fighting over damage done to a big projection of themselves into a large hunk of metal. If we didn't project so much of ourselves into material goods, we would need only one style of car, one style of clothing, one house design, and so on. But we need many different options because we are projecting different aspects of ourselves into and onto our surroundings.

If you are having any kind of difficulty in your life with a person or a situation, write down three words or phrases to describe the person or situation. Then write a paragraph or two about it and *own* your projections as just described. You will be able to recognize immediately what you have resisted seeing about yourself that is causing the "external" difficulty.

Any time we take the reins out of the hands of conditioning, it panics. In my observation, the people who realize they are something other than egocentricity often make that discovery when they decide to do something other than what egocentricity wants, and they feel the resulting panic.

For instance, let's say that I'm the kind of person who likes to keep my options open, go with the flow, and be spontaneous. I have no awareness that this identity enables egocentricity to pull me around in any direction at any moment. When ego says it doesn't like being somewhere, we leave. When ego doesn't want to do something, we don't do it. If I haven't yet noticed that there is someone talking and someone listening inside my head—that is, when a voice says, "I don't want to be here," I just assume it's me talking. People get frustrated with me because I change my mind a lot. I seem to be going along with some program, then suddenly I decide to go in another direction. Friends accuse me of not being committed, and I don't know what they're talking about, because this process is completely unconscious.

Then, through whatever combination of miracles and blessings, I decide I want to take up an awareness practice. I'm going to meditate. But I can't. Egocentricity says no, and I am incapable of going up against it. I can't do what I really want to do! It begins to dawn on me that I am not in control.

The fear that egocentricity throws into this situation is enough to send most people running for the cover of "life as we have known it." Conditioning reasserts its authority, the fear subsides, and unconsciousness prevails.

My encouragement is to pick one small thing that you want to change but know your conditioning does not support and try to change it—not because it's important to actually do it, but because it's a chance to watch how egocentricity attempts to thwart you. Seeing every step in egocentricity's process dramatically increases our ability to disidentify from our habitual attachment to, and support of, its program.

Seeing into the Issue by Examining Projection

Recognizing our projections is a quick way to see more deeply into the issue we want to work with.

What do I believe about other people/the world/life because I don't [work for myself]?

You may hear this kind of self-talk. "Other people are luckier, better, smarter, more talented, more selfish. It isn't fair. There's something wrong. It's not supposed to be this way. I'm being punished. I'm unworthy. This is preparing me for something better. I haven't yet opened up to my full potential. Maybe I don't want it enough. I need to work harder."

All of these are projections. I look out at the world from my conditioned viewpoint and project meaning onto everyone and everything based on my beliefs. If I believe it is only fair that I get what I want as a result of doing what I should do, when I don't get what I want after doing what I should do, life doesn't seem fair. My belief about fairness sets the standard for what is fair, and I project that standard onto every aspect of life. Whatever happens to me will be interpreted through my conditioned view of the world, and my perception will confirm my beliefs.

Notice that the line of demarcation is usually "getting what I want." If I get what I want, life is fair, other people are fair, every-

thing is as it should be, and nothing is wrong. I'm being rewarded, I have proof that I'm a good person, I'm doing the right thing,
and I'm going in the right direction. When I don't get what I
want, the conclusions are on the other end of the continuum, but
the result is the same—I'm right about the nature of reality.

CHAPTER NINE

DISIDENTIFICATION: The Crucial Shift

As mentioned previously, the process of social conditioning results in the formation of subpersonalities created to react to particular types of situations. Unfortunately, instead of identifying with a particular subpersonality only during the situation for which it is appropriate, we often remain identified with a subpersonality, carrying its responses into other situations, quite inappropriately. When an older sibling attempts to take a young child's food or toy, screaming and hitting serves a clear purpose for the young child. Continuing to rely on that response to get what one wants will, however, be distinctly disadvantageous in other situations.

Disidentification is the process of ceasing to act from unquestioned beliefs in a particular aspect of ourselves, whether that is a subpersonality or a role or any aspect of our identity. Disidentification can happen consciously or unconsciously.

Unconscious disidentification is an ongoing process for most of us. We move through the day shifting in and out of the various identities that make up the illusion of a separate self we think of as "I." As I wake up with my partner, I am a partner. I become a nurturing parent (or an impatient parent or any of a wide variety of types of parent) as I feed the kids and get them ready for the day. While getting ready for work, I assume a particular identity through what I choose to wear. At work, I become employee, boss, and co-worker, with an entire gamut of communication styles, emotional reactions, opinions, and moods to go with each role. As I go to lunch with a friend, call a potential client, do a little shopping, plan a weekend trip, or call my mother, I weave in and out of the various identities who make up "me." I don't notice that I am making these shifts as long as the shifts are correct. If I telephone Mom in my identity as loving daughter, all goes well. However, if the hard-driving business person calls Mom when Mom expects the loving daughter, things might not go as smoothly.

Most people who begin an awareness practice do so in large part because their conditioned identities are no longer serving them. This may not be a conscious thought, but dissatisfaction with one's survival strategies underlies the urge to pursue a path of greater freedom. People whose identities are blazing a wide path to success are rarely motivated to free themselves from their conditioning.

In my case, I realized that my raging temper was not leading me to the quality of life I wanted. As with most conditioned human beings, my conclusion was that life was not working because there was something wrong with me—in this case, my addiction to rage. If I would stop being that way, everything would be fine. But I could not stop being that way. I would gain a degree of consciousness *after* yet another temper tantrum. As I practiced awareness, I realized that I needed to become conscious earlier in the process. Soon I was able to be aware of it when I was in the tantrum. I would watch in horror as I raged. When I felt strong enough, I would force myself to stop.

After a while, I was able to do something very different from either being swept along in spite of myself or using the force of my will to control my behavior—I was able to disidentify. I was able to consciously choose to turn my attention *away* from the habitual patterns that fueled the temper and to turn my attention *to* my breath, enabling me to leave the identification with the raging personality and identify instead with the person who wanted to be rage-free.

So, conscious disidentification is choosing to bring awareness to our actions, becoming conscious of what aspects of our conditioning we are acting from, and moving away from that. When we disidentify, we can move to another aspect of our personality, or we can turn our attention to the breath and just be whatever we are in the moment.

Here's a testimonial for disidentification: *It feels so much better than the alternative.*

Using Awareness to Break False Connections

As we practice sitting still and focusing our attention, we move to increasingly subtle levels of awareness. We are able to notice a thought arise, detect an emotional reaction to the thought, and be aware of a conditioned behavior attached to the emotional reaction.

As we continue to observe, we become aware that these patterns do not vary. That thought, that emotion, and that behavior pattern always go together. As we attend more closely, we notice that there is a particular sensation that precedes the thought that triggers the emotion that leads to the behavior. (It is important to remember that the behaviors exist within us even when we are not acting them out. For instance, if I am angry with my partner and thinking about leaving, I imagine packing up and moving out without leaving a note—which is my conditioned behavior, even though I don't act on it.)

With practice, we can find the very first sensation—located in the epicenter, as discussed above—that initiates the conditioned chain of reactions. As we watch, we realize that that sensation, that movement in the body, does not *mean* what we assume it does, based on the ensuing chain of events. In fact, it does not mean anything; those two events—the sensation and the subsequent chain of reactions—have been connected to one another through a conditioned response and have no actual relationship other than that habitual linkage.

As we explore that phenomenon, we realize that the same thing has happened with the other links in the chain: That thought does not necessarily go with that sensation, that emotional reaction need not follow that thought, and that behavior is not invariably appropriate to that emotional reaction. As we practice disidentification, it's helpful to maintain an open, observant, questioning, but noncommittal attitude—best expressed, perhaps, by the ultimate Zen response, "Is that so?"

Personal Survey on Disidentification

- Can you see the importance of disidentification—of stepping back? How might disidentification assist you in getting where you want to go?

- Do you see that what is seen depends on what aspect of you is looking? How does this awareness affect your view of your life?

- Can you see how important it is to know exactly what's going on? How will looking to what *is* rather than to a conditioned belief system for information affect your view of yourself and your life?

- Can you see that this is not an intellectual understanding? How is your life different when you participate with your body, your emotions, and your spirit as well as your head?

- Do you realize that conditioned attempts to change are causing the situation to stay the same? What are some examples from your own life of egocentricity using an attempt to change as a way of keeping you stuck on the same merry-go-round?

- Can you see that only increasing your awareness can bring about the changes you seek?

Remember: You are looking for awareness in order to see more clearly the ways in which you have been conditioned. Your conditioning is not who you are. Please do not allow conditioning to use your awareness against you.

The Disidentified Perspective

The breath is our best tool for disidentification. We are usually so mesmerized by our conditioned identification—so caught up in the content, the drama of our story—that we have no perspective on the trap we are caught in.

Learning to turn the attention away from the thoughts, emotions, and survival strategies causes a break in the dramatic action. It is like cutting an audiotape with a pair of scissors. Clip. The tape has to be put back together before it can continue to play. The bad news for the audiotape, and the good news for us in our struggle against the hypnosis of conditioning, is that when it is put back together, it sounds funny. It sounds so odd that it catches one's attention each time it comes around. Clip. Another section sounds odd and catches our attention. Each time I come back to the breath, I am making that kind of clip in the continuous brainwashing loop that is my conditioning. I come back to the breath. Clip. I come back to the breath. Clip. The voices in my head are starting to catch my attention. Clip. Clip. Clip. I am hearing and seeing how the conditioning works.

I return to the breath, and when conditioning draws my attention back to itself, *I have a chance to see the whole system start up.* For a brief moment, it wasn't there, and now it is going to *come into existence.* I can watch *how* that happens. Time and time again, I can watch the programming not exist, feel the relief and expansiveness of the present, and then watch it reappear.

When I watch it from this disidentified perspective, it is not only *not* believable, it is ridiculous. The voices say utterly absurd things. I have believed them only because I was not present, because I was caught up in being a very small child who unquestioningly believed everything it was told.

Now, I'm disidentified, I'm watching. I am not that child, and I am not that conditioning. Clip. One breath at a time.

HELENE

Here's something I just saw in a moment of disidentification. The perfectionist in me holds these standards for me to be beautiful, brilliant, the best employee, even enlightened—whatever it is, I should be the best at it. Another part of me "knows" I'm not these things and I never will be. So for the first time, I questioned this voice that assumes I "should" be perfect—why do I need to be beautiful, brilliant, and acknowledged as the best employee? Can I love myself even if I'm ordinary? I think part of what's been driving me is that directive you talk about—someone set out an impossible task for me and expects me to finish it. So I keep waiting to get to the point where I'm doing things perfectly, without ever questioning the initial directive.

My issue for this class is how I do work, but I now see that this issue is with me in everything I do. In rela-

tionships, I look to others to show me that I am the things I think I should be—beautiful, brilliant, witty. Then I project disappointment onto them and feel hurt and embarrassed that they have discovered the real me. Either that, or I blame them for rejecting me, telling myself they don't see who I really am. At the same time, I hold ridiculous standards for them and fluctuate between trying to perpetuate an ideal image of them and being disappointed in them.

What if I got into a relationship knowing I'm ordinary and that the other person is ordinary? It never occurred to me before that being ordinary is just fine. What if I got a "satisfactory" rating rather than an "excellent" at work? It never occurred to me that that would be okay. I've always looked at women who are overweight, or whom I perceive as unattractive, who seem happy, and wondered how they could be.

It's amazing to me that as long as I've been practicing awareness, I've still let so many beliefs go unexamined. And the perfectionist is right here ready to beat on me for that. So what if I'm never enlightened, if I'm slow at this process, if I just keep plodding along, seeing what I see at the rate I see it, loving myself all the while? That would be just fine.

※   ※   ※

My response: Oh, that would be so much more than "just fine." It would be extraordinary. Bhagwan Shree Rajneesh was fond of pointing out that the most ordinary thing in the world is the desire to be extraordinary, and the most extraordinary thing is to be ordinary. We have judgments about people who are *merely existing*. We want to *live*. The problem is that we are so busy trying to live somewhere out in a future perfection, when we are as we should be and life is as it should be, that we miss the only life we have, which is here and now.

We must keep in mind that future and past are so important for egocentricity because egocentricity is an illusion and "exists" only in an illusory time. There is no place for an illusion of a separate self in "now." Nothing is separate "now." There are no boundaries or divisions "now." Conditioning is desperate to have us think about the past or the future, because in that fantasy realm, it appears to exist in its separateness.

CARLOS

For so many years, I've heard it and read it, over and over, that feelings are just energy, that we need to be aware of and accept them, without identifying with them. They are not who we are. And I never could do it. I could never believe it. When push came to shove, who else or what else was there for me to be? For decades, there has been no escape from the self-hating, self-hiding identifications, and the inner struggle and agitation, wheels spinning, lubricated with adrenaline, to somehow figure out how to make it better. Even sitting practice has been mostly excursions in fantasy. What I'm beginning to get is that this disidentification is something to actually practice.

❋   ❋   ❋

Yes, awareness *practice*. Like piano practice or football practice or dance practice. Over and over again, we come back to the breath. Again and again, we turn our attention away from where the habit of conditioning has taken it and back to the feeling of the breath in the body. Breathing all the way to the toes, all the way to the tips of the fingers, feeling the breath in the soles of the feet. Here. Right here.

Then—away wanders the attention, like the undisciplined toddler it is. Bring it back. Here. Now. Again and again, until the habit of unconscious wandering is ended. Over and over until the attention is happily residing here in this moment with awareness.

We Always Have a Choice

What keeps us from being able to make that simple movement away from our unconscious conditioned world and back to here, to this breath, to this moment, is the powerful grip that our conditioning has on us. It is relatively easy to come back to the breath when nothing is going on (and *relatively* is a big word in that sentence). But when we are up against something that is "real"—relationships, careers, or the two realest of the real, children and money—letting go and returning to the present-moment reality is no small matter.

For me, rage was real. It was more than just real—rage was *me*. On one memorable occasion, my little dog Toughie provided me with a big spiritual lesson: It is even possible to let go of what I considered a fixed, deep part of my identity.

Something had set me off—I have no idea what it was. (It's interesting to me that I can remember many, many of the rages—where I was, who was there, what I threw, what I broke—but I can't remember what a single one was about.) Whatever it was must have felt important, because I flew into a fury. I was screaming, yelling, throwing things, and as I whirled around to slam a chair into a corner, I saw Toughie right where the chair would have landed. Cowering in what must have seemed the most protected place available to her, the juncture of two walls, she had made herself as small as possible, and her eyes were filled with terror. Reflected in her eyes I saw the monster I had always believed myself to be.

In a blessed moment of clarity, I saw my behavior for what it was. I was throwing a temper tantrum, behaving like a two-year-old, and in the process, terrifying an innocent creature I loved. I saw the selfishness, the immaturity, the indulgence—but without any judgment.

I put the chair down and went over to Toughie. She recoiled from my touch. It was a heartbreaking moment. I told her that I understood she was afraid of me and I could certainly see why. That person I had been a few moments before was someone to be afraid of. I promised her that that was over, that never again would I frighten her like that. And I never did.

I would still get angry—you bet. But I never acted out that rage. I would feel the energy surge through my body, and then there would be a split second of remembering. It was as if a little voice reminded me, "You don't need to do it," and I would stop. I would go into a cleaning frenzy, chop a pile of wood, dig up a bed in the garden, or go for a long walk (Toughie's preference). But no raging.

In that process, I learned what willingness is. I realized that we always have all the willingness we need. We just need to examine what it is that we are willing to do. I had been willing to rage. Anger was my highest priority, although I would never have seen it or expressed it that way. When I had a higher priority— which was to disidentify, to free myself from conditioned suffering—I had all the willingness I needed to accomplish that.

Here is an example of that same kind of willingness:

SHARON

For about 20 years, I struggled with weight and compulsive eating. Every morning would start out the same, a mental rundown of what I had eaten the night before and a vow that I'd do better that day. I'd have great intentions until the evening, when I'd fall into the pattern of eating anything and everything until finally going to bed, disgusted, depressed, feeling like a weak and stupid person. The lowest point was when I sprayed perfume on the last half of a bag of cookies to prevent myself from eating the rest, then went back later to see if I could salvage any.

At some point, I realized that even though I thought I wanted to lose weight, deep down I knew I honestly didn't want to. Food meant too much to me, and I didn't want to give it up. When I felt bad, I ate to feel better. Food was my best friend. Once I saw that, I gave myself permission to wait until I really did want to lose the extra pounds.

The overeating had become a habit; I overate even when I felt good. It was the only way I knew to deal with feelings. At some point I realized that all I wanted was for the pain to cease. I wanted the focus on food to stop (what to eat, what not to eat, how to get control over the eating). I knew I was eating to cover something up. It became unimportant that I was overweight. I was willing to be overweight if I could just have peace of mind.

So, I let myself eat with no beatings afterward— I wanted to see what was going on. I just wanted to understand. Now I do, and miraculously, the weight is coming off. I can now be with myself no matter what I'm feeling, and eating is something I do when I'm hungry.

❊　❊　❊

A person will awaken and end suffering when they have suffered enough. Until that moment of having suffered enough, we dawdle, we rationalize, we indulge, we procrastinate, and we make excuses. When we have suffered enough, we get on with it.

When we make that decision to let the old ways go, we realize that we have everything we need for the process.

Gary Zukav says in his book *The Seat of the Soul* that when 10 percent of a person makes a decision such as waking up and ending suffering, 90 percent of the universe gets behind the person and the decision. I don't know where he gets his numbers, but they fit very well with my experience. Until we are truly committed, awareness, paying attention, clarity, sitting, disidentifying, and returning to center seem like impossible pursuits. Practice is hard and boring and awful. The whole mess is one big *should,* and the hapless victim of the requirement to end suffering slogs along in misery trying to do the right thing. But when you've suffered enough, when you are sick and tired of giving your life force to egocentric conditioning and its pack of hungry ghosts, awareness practice is a pure delight. It's coming home. It is a refuge and a relief.

Seeing into the Issue Through Disidentification

What would happen to the person I am now if I became someone who [works for myself]?

This is such an important piece of the puzzle. Elsewhere in the book, I talk about how "one process does not lead to another." We saw that concept in action with Ed in Chapter 5. By continuing to live out the process of feeling poor, he was unable to live into a process of feeling rich. I often tell people that if they want to be guaranteed a happy old age, it would behoove them to learn to be happy now. Instead, many people prepare for old age by being miserable now, being who they don't want to be, and doing what they don't want to do in order to save for their retirement. But having a lot of money when you retire is not going to turn you into a happy person. "Yeah, but if I didn't have to go to work, I'd automatically be happy!" Really? Are you sure? Maybe that would be a good thing to find out about, because if that belief is not true (and I am here to say it is not), then *now* will be miserable, and *then* will be miserable, too.

Does this mean that we shouldn't work? That we shouldn't save money? That we shouldn't be responsible? No, of course it doesn't. What it means is that we shouldn't confuse issues.

HOME SWEET HOME

The Fullers wanted desperately to move into a larger house. With three kids, a dog, and a cat, there were just too many bodies for that sweet little house that they started out in when it was just the two of them. They worked, they cut corners, they scrimped and saved, and finally they were able to move into the house of their dreams: five bedrooms, three baths, a family room plus a living room, and a master bedroom with its own mini-kitchen. If you had told them ahead of time that they wouldn't be happy there, they would have thought you were crazy. But unhappy they were.

They felt like strangers. They felt as if they needed to make an appointment to see one another. It was too big, it felt cold, it wasn't homey. They missed the old neighborhood, their friends, their favorite restaurants and places to shop.

❋ ❋ ❋

Did the Fullers make a mistake? Probably not. In time, they will adjust to the larger space, make new friends, figure out how to stay connected with their old friends, find new favorite places, and no doubt fill up that huge house until it feels cozy. Their anguish could have been avoided, however, if they had realized that one process does not lead to another—that *wanting* doesn't lead to satisfaction. Having a new house doesn't mean you won't miss old friends. Having more room is going to have a big impact on how people live together. Loving a new house doesn't mean you won't grieve the loss of the old one.

So, what will happen to the person I am now when I work for myself? If I lose sight of the fact that life lived fully is a process of expansion, if I don't bring conscious awareness to all the changes in me, my old identity (my childhood survival system) will become threatened, and that old me will assert itself in an attempt to once again gain control of life. When people report that process to me, their stories often include illness, depression, anxiety, and the failure of the new direction.

In the next chapter, I will describe some memorable instances in my monastic training when I learned to "let go." For now, let me reassure you that nothing can harm you as a result of releasing old patterns and moving into a freer way of life. Letting go is not the same as getting rid of. Letting go is allowing what *is* to simply *be,* without clinging or pushing away.

Life is a constant process of change. It is ironic that many of us work so hard to change those things we have been conditioned to believe need to be changed, while at the same time furiously resisting the natural changes that life brings. We want everything to stay the same except those things we want to change. As we relax into the acceptance that life is living itself and the wisdom of understanding that that requires no effort from us, we can be more comfortable with the unfolding of our lives.

Most of us would probably agree that it would not be a good idea to plant a garden and then go out each day to help the plants along by giving them a tug up out of the earth. The plants know how to grow. The changes that happen within the plant to take it from seed to maturity are natural, built in, and function perfectly. The same is true with us, when we aren't getting those "helpful" tugs in the "right" direction from egocentric conditioning.

If I haven't been working for myself because I have been afraid to take full responsibility for my own financial success or failure, *and now I know that*, I can be grateful to a very intelligent survival system that defended me until I felt ready to go out on my own. I don't have to feel bad about my conditioning, or hate it, or try to annihilate it. It has been with me a long time and has served me in ways I will probably never know about. Instead of an execution, how about a job change for that part of me that has kept me safe in my ability to make a living?

If that part of me needs something to be concerned about, something to take care of, I could ask it to be in charge of my relationship with my in-laws. That is a relationship that needs careful, conscientious, near-paranoid attention. Attending to family would be a good job for someone with a well-developed be-careful-worry-about-the-future-belt-and-suspenders approach to life. These are good skills. Why not use them to my benefit?

As I feel more able to operate without the benefit of conditioning, the survival systems will feel less triggered, and the tasks assigned to my defense systems can be smaller and less significant.

All of this requires a good deal of paying attention and conscious awareness, but when confronted with that concern, I like to remind myself that there is nothing better that I could be doing with my life. Attention and awareness take no extra time or energy. I can have my attention and awareness either on my conditioning or in the present moment. I can promise you this: Life is far better in every way when attention and awareness are in the present.

CHAPTER TEN

CENTER:
Home Free

Center is a word we use to describe a present-moment life experience. We talk about "being centered" or "at center," "coming back to center," and "centering." However, in any discussion of *center*, it quickly becomes apparent that no one can say exactly what that term means. Even those who think they know the experience have trouble describing it. "There is a feeling of well-being, nothing is wrong, everything is all right just as is"— that's the kind of thing you are likely to hear.

At that point, some people get uncomfortable. "But everything is not all right. People are starving, children and animals are being abused. How can you say everything is all right, when so much is obviously wrong?"

That is a very good question that takes us back to the beginning of this book. Early on we looked at how human beings have the possibility of living in either of two worlds, the conditioned world of egocentricity and suffering, or a world free of suffering, which is the experience of *center*.

In the first case, we are identified with fear, loss, deprivation, a feeling/belief that there is something wrong, resistance, urgency, defensiveness, isolation, loneliness, judgment of others, self-judgment, beliefs and opinions, being right, criticism of others, self-criticism, punishment, worry, anxiety, greed, delusion, insecurity, superiority, inferiority, tension, boredom, indulgence, resentment, discomfort, shame, the illusion of control, guilt, blame, unworthiness, and confusion.

In the second case, there is ease, well-being, sufficiency, openness, acceptance, expansiveness, compassion, and even joy in experiencing the nonseparateness of being present, here and now.

Our conditioning would tell us that we cannot accept the present because that would mean accepting all that is wrong. It would be irresponsible, uncaring, cold, and cruel to accept the suffering of the world.

The difficulty here is that we are conditioned to view *accept* as a synonym for *condone* or *agree*. We assume that accepting that people are starving would mean that we don't care; it is all right with us that people are starving.

No wonder people line up on the side of resisting acceptance! But, as is often the case, our words and concepts are being used in the service of conditioning. *Accept* in this context simply means *acknowledge*, as in "I accept that the car is red." I don't need to have any opinion about it; it is simply a matter of our agreeing that the word we use to describe that color is *red*.

I would suggest that certain aspects of life are kept in the "unacceptable" category—not because finding them unacceptable enables us to change them, but because finding them unacceptable enables us to maintain them. "I refuse to accept that people are starving!" That may sound noble in some circles, but where does it leave us? Regrettably, it seems that often we feel we are doing our part to "right the wrongs" by railing against the "wrongs." It can *feel* as if one is doing a great deal because a lot of energy is being expended. But hating hunger is not feeding anyone except egocentricity.

Here is a Zen story about a fellow who went to train in a monastery. (We must keep in mind here that most of us who go to train in a monastery feel ourselves to be authorities on the subject of right and wrong and how things should be.)

> *On the first morning, this man strode purposefully up the steps of the meditation hall, and as he bowed deeply, he noticed off to one side of the door a mop and a bucket of dirty water. He stiffened slightly, somewhat shocked at the carelessness of leaving something so filthy outside the meditation hall door. He entered the hall and went to his place to sit, and forgot about it.*
>
> *As he entered the hall the next day, bowing deeply, he again spied the mop and bucket. He stopped mid-bow. What in the world? How could this be possible in a Zen monastery? Zen is known for order, precision, and attention to detail. Shaking his head he entered the hall, went to his place to sit, and forgot about it.*
>
> *The next morning, he was on the lookout for the mop and bucket, and there they were. "What kind of place is this? Maybe Zen isn't all it's cracked up to be. What kind of people are these anyway? This is unacceptable! Why isn't someone taking care of that mess?" He entered the hall and went to his place to sit, but he remain troubled.*
>
> *The next day and the next and the next, the mop and bucket were there. Finally, one day as the man passed by the meditation hall and saw the same sight at the door, he smiled. He climbed the steps, picked up the mop and bucket, carried them off, and took care of them.*

Now, if he had remained committed to his position of "that is unacceptable," the dirty mop and bucket might still be there! The first step in taking care of the situation is accepting that it is, indeed, there. "Yes, I accept the fact that the mop and bucket of filthy water is there." I do not have to like its presence, do not need to agree that it is in a good place, and do not have to figure out whose fault it is or what it means. Once again, my opinion about the placement of the bucket is irrelevant to anything *except my suffering.*

If it is wrong that the bucket is where it is, if it should not be there, if someone is wrong for leaving it there, if its presence means something about the people or the place, if it makes them wrong and me right, if it places me in opposition to them and makes them *other,* suffering is bound to follow.

Could I, would I clean up the mess if I did not hold opinions about how things should be? We are conditioned to believe we would not. We are conditioned to believe that only our judgment and punishment causes us to do the "right" thing. I would suggest that our judgment and punishment causes us to do the suffering thing.

We assume that if we accepted everything as it is (read "did not care"), nothing would ever happen. Not true. Not even close to true. Why? Because when we are not separate, there is nothing that is not *us.*

The fellow in the story was paralyzed by his opinions. He was so busy hating the presence of the mop and bucket and reinforcing his beliefs and assumptions that he could not act. Again, we assume that without conditioned opinions, we would not notice that the meditation hall entrance is not a suitable place for a mop and a bucket of dirty water. Conditioning would argue that, all things being equal, the meditation hall entrance is as good a place as any for anything. That is a false position. Here is something that each person must experience for themselves: Nature does not make unsightly messes; only egocentrically conditioned human beings do.

When we are in the moment, nothing is pushing us to leave something undone. Ah, ego would argue, isn't that just another belief? Again, you must see for yourself. Can you imagine cleaning your house *for the house?* Can you imagine washing your car to honor the car?

When we are not separate, there is nothing that is separate from us. The meditation hall, the mop and bucket, and the meditator are simply what is—all one *suchness*. There is nothing wrong with any of it, and I can clean the bucket *for the bucket*. I can put it away because it feels good to put it away—for the bucket, for the meditation hall, and for everyone who enters the hall, including me.

In accepting everything as is, there is no resistance, no other, no object in relation to which "I" must be a separate subject. My life experience is one of "we." I am home, I belong here, I fit in— as does everything. Life is a one that cannot be divided. There cannot be anything wrong, because there is no alternative to what is.

❊   ❊   ❊

We sit in meditation to return to oneness.

I sit down on the cushion, and my mind wanders. The voices in my head begin to tell me that I can't meditate, look at the state of my mind. I can't stay focused on the breath for a moment. I'm a mess. I'm distracted, undisciplined. I listen to the voices and bring my attention back to the breath. My mind wanders. I return to the breath. My arm itches, I don't scratch, I bring my attention back to the breath. The voices tell me this is stupid, a waste of time, meant for people with less to do than I. I gently bring my attention back to the breath. My back hurts. Patiently I return my attention to the breath.

It is all fine. Everything is okay—the wandering attention, the voices, the beliefs, the self-hate—it is all okay. All of it is. Nothing to do about it. Nothing wrong that needs to be righted. This is what is.

Slowly, patiently, I am learning to accept what is as it is. And here is the huge, wonderful, amazing secret to the whole thing: If there is no one who believes themselves to be separate from what is, no one to find something wrong with what is, no one to make a problem out of what is in order to have something to do, then *there is no problem.*

Acceptance

To return for a moment to the starving people, here is what I think would happen with world hunger if we practiced acceptance rather than hatred: We would feed people. Instead of our time, energy, and resources going toward maintaining egocentric attitudes, we could turn all of it toward feeding people. Why do we not? Because acceptance does not serve egocentric social conditioning.

As I sit still in meditation, with acceptance, I hear the voices for what they are. I don't need to hate myself for having them, I don't need to fight them, and I don't need to try to get rid of them. As I realize that they are simply making my life miserable, I turn my attention away from them and back to the ease and comfort of breathing. I watch the conditioned opinions, beliefs, and assumptions arise, and see the suffering they cause in my life and in the lives of others. I don't have to hate my conditioning; I don't have to punish myself for having been conditioned. I can just gently bring my attention back to the refuge of the breath. The mind wanders, sensations arise, emotions pass through, and I continue to breathe, right here, right now, in this moment. There is no resistance to anything; everything can be exactly as it is, including this human being who is blessed with this front-row seat at the amazing spectacle that is a human life.

For those people whose inner voices are screaming, "But there's so much to do! How can I get anything done if all I'm doing is accepting?"—remember, *doing* is the battle cry of egocentricity. It keeps us in a state of urgency so we will continue to *do.* In Hindu philosophy, we hear, *No deed there is, no doer thereof.* Life lives. Life does not need an illusion of a separate self to make it happen. In the moment, there is everything to do, and the one who is doing it is not separate from it.

An ancient saying by Sengtsan, the Third Zen Patriarch, that can comfort us as we try to wean ourselves from urgency and settle ourselves into the comfort of nonseparate acceptance, is: *Don't seek after enlightenment; simply cease to cherish opinions.*

We long for conditions, internal and external, to be as we wish—not because of the conditions, but because when everything is the way we want it to be, we have a momentary respite from the dissatisfaction of that self who is in opposition to life. For a moment or so, we feel relieved by the absence of resistance. It is good to remember that that absence of resistance and the joyful relief that absence provides is available to us in each moment we are here, in this moment, present, at center.

Waking Up

To me, the ultimate spiritual question is: *Who am I following?* The thoughts that just passed through my mind—where did they come from? What is guiding me through life? Is it authenticity, true nature, all that is, the present moment? Or is it egocentricity, conditioning, a subtle yet urgent hungry ghost?

The Buddha began the journey that led to his profound awakening when he realized that life inevitably results in old age, sickness, and death. People, creatures, all forms of life everywhere are dying as I write this, are dying as you read this. That we die is not in question. How we will die—how we will live—is up to us. For me, the issue of how I live and how I die is of paramount importance.

These are huge questions we are looking into. Today is the day to face them. There is no comfort, nothing to be gained, in postponing the inevitable. As the Buddha advised us just before his death, we must each work out our own salvation diligently.

The best time to work out our own salvation is now.

And it isn't easy, is it? I think the worst part of this work—well, one of the worst parts, anyway—is that it takes so much time, so much pain, so much suffering to get to the point of being willing to do the work that needs to be done to let go what we're clinging to that has caused our suffering. Once we have seen what we do that causes our suffering and we are willing to stop, isn't that enough? Shouldn't it be clear sailing from that point? But no, we have to keep sitting in awareness, being still, staying present, attending closely—and our reward is to keep going through the circumstances that got us to the point of having suffered so much that we were willing to stop doing what we had been doing so we could stop suffering!

To create a picture of our plight as human beings, trying to wake up out of this miasma of conditioned suffering into conscious, compassionate awareness, the Buddha used an image of a long silk scarf into which a series of knots have been tied. We attempt to turn in a different direction when we can't manage to tie one more knot in the silk scarf that is our life.

ANDREA

As I have been seeing through layers of conditioning, the issue of wanting someone to love me who doesn't love me has given way to a more central issue of how I leave myself, how I abandon myself, for the love of someone else. For now, I am sitting with this and crying a lot. The epicenter is the tears. I can bring up an image, cry, and go back to the breath.

As I do this, I recognize a very young part of me who does not understand. Why, if you love someone, do they not love you? Why, if you love someone, do they leave you for someone else? Why, if you love someone, do they die?

And then, an occasional brilliance shines through from that place of compassionate awareness, and I can stay with and reassure this very young part of myself about this lovely and mysterious and fragile tenderness of love and of life. This makes me cry a lot. Sometimes it feels like letting go. Other times I know I am identified with another part of me who wants something outside of myself. I keep experimenting, asking myself questions, such as what is this feeling here and now I am trying to escape? I keep getting answers, returning to the breath, to sitting, to a glimpse of compassionate awareness and that feeling in the body that just knows.

❈　❈　❈

This is a variation on another image the Buddha used to symbolize our situation in this world of suffering: We are like children playing in a burning building. We are so caught up in our games that we have no idea that the whole structure is getting ready to come down on us, crushing us, consuming us in flames. In the account related above, someone is willing to go into that burning building and rescue the child who will be crushed under the collapsing building. Will a rescue be possible? Is it too late? We cannot know. What we know is that, regardless of how frightening and painful it may be, we have to try. When we reach a certain point in our awareness, going in is less frightening and painful than not going in.

It is easy, when life is feeling difficult, to allow conditioning to pull our attention into all that is "wrong." The voices begin with a long list of complaints. I don't like this. I hate that. Why is it that way? What is the matter with them? On and on and on. The sound of it is so old and familiar that it's like a lullaby. We nod off, and the hungry ghosts tuck into another meal of the vitality that animates our lives. What can break the spell?

The best two antidotes I know to that unconscious conditioned suffering are gratitude and compassion. One of our monks has a practice that assists him in freeing himself from egocentricity and returning to the present. Instead of allowing conditioning to remind him of what is wrong, he practices remembering all the blessings he has. He simply says "thank you"—over and over, with every breath. Each time his attention moves to something new, each time he sees or smells or hears something, he says "thank you." If an attack of conditioning is particularly virulent, he *writes* "thank you." He tells me he sometimes has to write pages of thank you's before the grip of conditioning is broken.

Other monks have told me that nature is their escape from the clutches of egocentricity. You may have noticed that when conditioning has you, when you're identified with an unpleasant aspect of the self, it is very difficult to focus on anything pleasant. Someone tells a joke, but it's not funny. Someone says something uplifting, and you think they're a jerk. Someone offers a fun activity, but you're not interested. "No, I'm going to go home and do nothing." It takes a strenuous focus of attention to stay stuck in misery, but egocentricity is always willing to make the effort! If you have a glimpse of a larger perspective and can get out into nature, conditioning will have a harder time maintaining its hold. Just looking up at the sky, contemplating a tree, or listening to a bird can break the grip of conditioning.

Are these permanent solutions? No. They are practices. Temporary experiments. When you feel yourself come back to here and now, take a long deep breath, let it all go, and for just a moment, *be.*

Practice in Centering

These exercises are an easy way to practice dropping conditioned patterns and moving into center. With each exercise, take a few moments to go into the memory as fully as you are able. Take your time, and explore each before going on to the next. In your imagination, engage all your senses. Feel the air, the sun, or the rain; recall the colors and the textures around you; hear the breeze or the birds or the people. Let your self be completely in the scene you are remembering.

Take a few long, full breaths and see if you can let go of everything else. Breathing in, breathing out.

Recall a time when you were in a place of great physical beauty.

Recall a time when someone was kind to you.

Recall a time when you were filled with love for someone or something.

Recall a favorite piece of music.

Recall a time when you felt loved.

We can't feel the love, compassion, and gratitude that bring beauty and joy to our lives as long as our time, energy, and attention are in service to egocentricity. The illusion of a separate self wants and needs to survive. Love, compassion, gratitude, beauty, and joy—because they don't need to "survive"—are threatening to egocentricity. There has to be something wrong so there is something urgent to do, something to survive; and well-being, satisfaction, peace, generosity, and loving-kindness do not signal that something is wrong. The biggest piece of awareness practice is learning to drag our attention back from our obsession with how things are and how they should be—what's wrong, who is to blame, and what we should do.

Love, compassion, gratitude, beauty, joy, well-being, satis-faction, peace, generosity, and loving-kindness are there when we stop doing everything else. Those are words for what is there when the illusory world of conditioning, the sense of a separate self, falls away.

Egocentric conditioning will tell us that we are doing aware-ness practice wrong precisely *because* we are on the right track and it feels threatened. How slippery and subtle this egocentric conditioning is! We are so foolish to try to fight it. If we would simply follow it around watching how it does its dirty work (and we might be truly awed by that), we would be way ahead of the game. Instead, we feel bad about what it projects onto us, we go unconscious, and we lose before the game even begins.

It is true that as spiritual practice deepens, fear increases. Egocentricity, karmic conditioning, the illusion of a separate self, and suffering are one and the same, and the way they feel to us is what we call fear. When the control of conditioning is threatened, conditioning reacts with more fear. Sadly, we have learned to identify so strongly with conditioning that we assume it is our-selves who fear, and we go into defensive maneuvers that condi-tioning has learned to use to protect itself. At the very moment when we could turn away from conditioning and leave it without the support it needs to continue to rule our lives, we identify with it and rush to its rescue.

However, as with all tyrants, eventually conditioning goes too far. It crosses a line, and we begin to see that it is not taking care of us, it is taking care of itself at our expense. At that moment, we have an opportunity to withdraw our devotion to its cause—and that is as scary as can be. Conditioning will pull out all the stops to get us back. Death, destruction, annihilation, the loss of all we hold dear—we are threatened that every hideous thing we can imagine will happen if we don't return to the fold and give all our attention and energy to conditioning.

You can learn to hold out. Practice enables you to sit on your cushion and just keep breathing until conditioning has done its worst and you are still alive and yourself. Of course it will continue to threaten. "You just wait. This was nothing; next time it will be worse." Idle threats: If fear had had anything scarier to hit you with, it would have done so. Ride out the storm, and when it has hit you with its best shot and you're still standing—or in this case, sitting—you will have taken a step toward freedom that cannot be wrested from you by anything in the world.

Every ego wants exactly the same thing: to be special, to have sympathy, to be first, to be better, to get more . . . add your own wants. Everyone shares that same egocentric conditioning. It is possible for us to stop clinging to whatever is egocentric, to cease dragging around a childish version of the ideal adult life, and to drop all that is limited and step into the freedom and originality of authenticity.

Seeing Through the Illusion

My favorite way of talking about most attempts to do something about oneself is, "As long as you are improving yourself, you will always have a self to improve." Egocentricity wants its own existence regardless of the program it is required to endure. For example, I will speak now as your ego. You decide to quit eating so much sugar. That's not a problem for me. While you're eating sugar, I can make your life miserable about sugar. If you stop, I can make you miserable about *not* having sugar. In fact, misery, not sugar, is what *I* feed on. Remember the hungry ghosts?

This practice most emphatically is *not* a process of self-improvement. This work is based on the premise that regardless of what you were taught to believe, there never was anything wrong with you. Since there never has been anything wrong with you, there is nothing that needs to be fixed or improved. What we are learning to see clearly are all the false ideas and assumptions that cause us to believe that we are separate selves with whom there is something wrong. The most difficult piece of this to comprehend is that "you" don't suffer—what suffers is the illusion of a separate self.

An illusion of a separate self is very difficult to maintain without the illusion of something wrong about which something must be *done*. Doing is the life-blood of egocentricity. Doing is what egocentricity always uses to throw us off the scent when we're onto its nefarious deeds. There you are, sitting, watching, seeing clearly, seeing *through*, and egocentricity wails, "But what do I *do?*" "Oh, right," we answer in a daze, "I should be doing something." And off we stagger in a fog of confusion. Don't fall for it. Just sit still and watch it. (Remember that "sitting still" is what we call conscious, compassionate awareness, paying close attention—it's not just when you're sitting on the meditation cushion.)

If there is nothing wrong, there is nothing urgent that needs to be done, and life just *is*. Suffering is the result of wanting something to be other than the way it is, of believing something is wrong, and of trying to do something. Just breathing, life is.

Does this mean that all activity must stop if you are not going to be a separate self who *does*? No. All of nature lives just fine without holding a belief that there is something wrong with it that needs to be fixed. Trees don't stand around and compare heights. A flower doesn't automatically wilt when it notices that another flower has a different color or a fancier blossom. They go right on growing and blooming and treeing and flowering—and we can see that they are wonderful exactly as they are. Same with people. Life will live us perfectly exactly as we are, if we let go of our better ideas and simply let it.

Personal Survey on Acceptance

- Imagine completely accepting the issue you are working with.

- What would this issue look like if you had no opinions about it?

- What would happen to the issue if everything about it were okay with you?

- What would happen to this issue if you viewed it as a learning experience?

- What would this issue look like if all your emotions were acceptable?

- What would happen if feelings were just feelings and didn't *mean* anything?

- What if there were nothing wrong with any of this, or with you?

Acceptance is the answer. Resistance has been keeping the structure in place. With acceptance, resistance falls away. Without resistance, the structure collapses. When the structure collapses, we are free.

Letting Go

When I first went to the monastery to train, I was given the job of building an altar for the meditation hall. My teacher knew that I had grown up being the eyes for a blind father who had taught me carpentry, and that I had been building things since before I started school.

For the altar, I was given two sheets of plywood, a hand saw, some finish nails, a hammer, and a container of carpenter's glue. I had already learned enough to know that in a Zen monastery, certainly in this one, the wise course was to accept the materials, bow, and get on with it.

Now, for those of you not versed in the building arts, plywood is not the customary wood of choice for fine furniture. Plywood is not pretty and is not meant to be seen. Plywood goes *under* things. An altar out of plywood? Holy rockets!

I commenced my work, and before long had a truly ugly plywood box with a sloping top, made to specifications. I asked my teacher what kind of finish I should put on it, assuming we would use some sort of stain and try to pretend that the "grain" was attractive. He said he would like it to be painted, and therefore it would need to have a smooth, well-sanded surface. That is not possible with plywood, but he had a solution before I posed the problem: I would cover the "altar"—as we were managing, with straight faces, to call it—with spackle. That way it could be sanded smooth and made ready for the paint.

Again, for those of you who aren't home-project oriented, spackle is what you use to fill in little holes, like nail holes, in sheetrock. "Little" is the operative word; spackle is for little jobs, little spaces, little cracks—not great hulking boxes made from plywood. Spackle was never intended to cover 50 or so square feet of unattractive material.

Three large containers of spackle and countless sheets of sandpaper later, the altar was ready to paint. The paint arrived: orange—bright, garish, awful orange. Those years of practice in keeping a poker face regardless of the circumstances really paid off in that moment.

I painted the altar orange. It never appeared in the meditation hall. The last time I saw it, it was upside down in the tool shed, filled with spare plumbing parts. I thought it had found a much better purpose than the one for which it had ostensibly been intended.

My next assignment was to make a copy of our Daily Recollection, which is recited each morning. I was told to make the copy in calligraphy, and it was suggested that I would turn out something as fine as a hand-decorated medieval Bible. Why not? The fact that I had no experience with calligraphy was not a problem. When I purchased the pens and ink, I picked up a how-to book on calligraphy. I spent many, many hours struggling to produce an acceptable copy of the Daily Recollection. Some of those hours were frustrating because I thought I should be able to do the job and do it well and end up with a certain result. At other times, I was completely relaxed—when I knew my standards for the job were impossible to meet, and I sensed a higher purpose behind my teacher's stated objective. In the end, my calligraphic copy of the Daily Recollection was surpassed in sheer ugliness only by the orange altar.

By the time my teacher suggested that I would lead awareness workshops, I felt pretty confident that it would be another do-this-so-you-can-see-how-you-do-this adventure. Off I went with another monk. She was a born teacher, eager to lead classes and workshops on any subject. The workshops were interactive. The participants were led through guided imagery exercises, then they were asked to answer questions, write down observations, and engage in various forms of "sharing."

I lived in dread of the sharing. My co-facilitator would practically rub her hands together in gleeful anticipation as she asked the participants, "Who would be willing to share?" My main contribution was sitting there in silence, keeping the meditation cushion warm and trying not to look too terrified.

It was usually the first evening of a two-day workshop before I could manage to open my mouth and get a few words out. My face would be bright red, my voice would be quivering, and I would be shaking so hard that I could barely stay on my cushion.

I hated it. Nothing but my love of Zen practice could have made me endure that torture.

But I knew what I had signed on for. It had taken me a year and a half to talk my teacher into letting me enter the monastery, and before he agreed to accept me, he had said, "I will find all your buttons and push them. I will find everything you cannot stand, and I will rub your nose in it." Who could resist an offer like that? And here it was: something I really couldn't stand.

I knew that my aim was to see through the grip that egocentric conditioning had on my life. And I knew that as ugly as egocentricity was, letting go of it was not going to be easy or fun or pleasant in any way. I was willing to do whatever it took, but I hated it.

One day, after many months of the regular torture of leading workshops, our teacher called my co-facilitator and me in for a conference. Looking at the other monk, he said, "You will no longer be leading the weekend workshops." Her face fell. A spark of hope ignited in my chest—then died a quick death when he turned to me and said, "You will be doing the workshops by yourself from now on."

There have been times in my life when I spent sleepless nights filled with anxiety and terror, nights in which all I could do was sit on my meditation cushion, holding on to it for dear life, knowing that it was the only thing between me and stark staring madness—but none was worse than that night. What was I going to do? There were only two responses to a request from my teacher: a deep bow signifying agreement, or a deep bow meaning good-bye.

I sat in front of him the next day, knowing that my life was over. I could not do what he was asking, and I could not say no to him. I had hit a new level of suffering.

"Roshi," I began, "please understand, it is not that I am unwilling. I *can't* do it. I don't know how. I don't have the skills or the aptitude or the knowledge. I cannot do it." Through that whole little speech, I was unable to look at him. It was hard to get the words out because with each one, a new flood of tears poured down my face. I sat there sobbing in misery until the tears subsided. He hadn't said a word, so I thought maybe I should try again. I looked up at him, ready to gauge his reaction to my misery.

He was looking at me with what I finally was able to name compassion. I had never seen that look on a human face, had never seen it filling human eyes. With more tenderness than I had ever felt coming from another person before or since, he said to me, "You will do for the love of others what you would never be willing to do for yourself."

I could barely take it in. I was not being punished—this was not something that was being done *to* me; this was being done *for* me.

The fact that I was willing to continue facilitating workshops (as a condition of being allowed to continue monastic training) did not make the process any easier. I continued to be plagued by self-consciousness at my lack of ability. Sometimes the voices of self-hate would make the drive home after a weekend nearly unbearable. "Why did you say that?" "You didn't even remember to answer that question." "They all think you're an idiot!"

It was completely horrible—and the best awareness practice I have ever had the privilege of doing. I knew that coming back to the breath was my only escape from the relentlessness of the voices. The breath, the present moment as refuge, became real to me for the first time. I could see that the voices were not trying to help me, that they were not on my side, nor were they giving me information to make me better. They were mean and hateful and aimed at making me miserable. Perhaps at another time in my life the voices would have been able to convince me that if I were to stop doing the workshops, they would stop beating me up, that it was only because I was so abysmal at facilitating that they said the kinds of things they said to me. But their timing was off. I knew that I was trying harder than I had ever tried with anything in my life, and instead of encouragement, all I got was abuse.

My willingness to continue to do the work grew daily. I realized that seeing through egocentric conditioning was my only hope, and I could see that awareness worked. Moment by moment, I proved to myself that suffering happened only when I was distracted, pulled out of the moment and into the world of conditioning. If I could stay *here* and be in the moment I was in, suffering was not possible. I no longer had to *believe* that if I did the work of paying attention, I would end suffering—I was giving myself irrefutable proof.

Then the truly miraculous awareness happened. I began to see that if I did not look to conditioning to provide the information I needed for someone in a workshop—if I would just be still, breathe, and allow whatever might arise to arise—I would feel a clarity. In that clarity, the information the participant needed would be there. I would open my mouth to speak and often have no idea what I was going to say until I heard myself say it. It was astounding! It would have been spooky, except that it felt so right, so natural. Not to mention the fact that each time it happened, the participant responded with a slightly stunned look of, "Yes—oh, yes, that's right."

There was no mystery about whether my responses came from egocentricity or the present moment. When I looked to egocentricity for a response, a person might acknowledge that what I said was true for them, but the exchange had a feel of teacher-and-student-in-a-classroom, dry, dead, old, and rehashed. I was speaking from something I "knew" to be true. "If you come back to the breath, live in the breath, suffering is not possible," I could say. Yawn. I nod, the participant nods. Yes, we agree that is so. Buddhists say it. Christians say it in other language. Hindus know it. Uh-huh.

But when a response arose from that deeper clarity of being with what is in the moment, we could have been talking about the relative merits of whole wheat and white bread, and the words still resonated with a depth of truth that often left us awed. "In the zone." Here/now. This. Circle with no remainder. Aaahhhhhh, with no one to say "aaahhhhhh."

These were exhilarating, terrifying steps to be taking. When it worked, it was the highest experience I had ever had. And there were moments when it didn't work. There were times when I would open my mouth and there was nothing there to say. Horror. The desire to run back to the tried-and-true-going-to-the-conditioned-head for answers was nearly overwhelming. To sit there feeling utterly foolish, knowing people were, in fact, wondering about my mental abilities, to find the willingness to continue in those situations—well, it challenged my commitment to awareness practice as nothing else has.

I took a great deal of comfort from one of my favorite New Testament stories. Jesus sent the disciples out to preach. The environment was hostile, and the disciples were afraid. What if they were arrested? What if they were put in jail? What should they do? What should they say? Jesus encouraged them to take no thought for what they would say, for when the time came, what they needed would be given to them.

Of course, the New Testament story does not speak to the situation of giving no thought to what one would say and then nothing being "given" after all. But I was not confused about the value of that experience: It speaks directly to taking egocentricity out of the driver's seat in the vehicle of life. What suffered when I didn't have some brilliant rejoinder for a sincere student of awareness practice? Only my ego. Humiliation is an experience that only egocentricity has, and from my perspective, it is the only thing that really needs the experience. It is extraordinarily important to understand that egocentricity is not capable of the brilliant clarity that is there when the illusion of a separate self is not.

I made a vow to my teacher and to myself that no one would ever ask me a second question about something that I had failed to look into as closely as I could after the first time the question was asked. I may never have considered that question until some-one else brought it up, but I will have explored its depths by the time it's brought up again. That's the best I could offer—and it still is.

✳ ✳ ✳

It is a frightening prospect to be confused about whether ego-centricity or the clarity of the present moment is the source for action. If I were to have some sort of "enlightenment experience," or worse, "think" that I had an enlightenment experience without being clear about what is ego and what is the absence of ego, I could be a very dangerous person.

My teacher would talk to me often and at length about the influence anyone in a teacher's role has in the life of a student. Of course, such influence exists not only in a student-teacher rela-tionship, but in any relationship in which the "power" of the two individuals is out of balance. Doctors or therapists with patients, adults with children, coaches with athletes are all relationships with an imbalance of power. My teacher would counsel me to be watchful and ever careful not to be an undue influence in any-one's life. People are grateful to the person who gives to them what they believe they do not possess. In their gratitude, they feel that they owe a debt, and they wish to repay that debt with what-ever they believe has comparable value—their money, their pos-sessions, and even their bodies.

So, I used to pray that I would never be confused about my own spiritual attainment. I had a horror that someday someone would be sitting in front of me as I had sat in front of my teacher, and I would fail them through some attachment to egocentricity that had not been there with him as he guided me. His selfless-ness continues to be the beacon that directs my practice, his example of commitment constantly pushing me to face the repugnant, accept the unacceptable, and not settle for what I've seen so far.

How am I doing? Remember that essential spiritual question: *Who am I following in life, authenticity or egocentricity?* Here is what I'm learning. The one who wants to know the answer to that sort of question is in the latter club. That which is present to *what is,* is in the former.

I cannot know, can't get a guarantee—all I can do is the very best I can to drop whatever I am clinging to rather than being present and coming back to this moment. I trust that all I seek is right here and now. I don't have to hope that is true—I have had the experience. What I can practice is returning to *this*, recognizing the compassion of all that is, and feeling gratitude for the momentous opportunity that is life.

The release, the freedom, we are seeking is not available to us as long as we cling to our egocentric, conditioned ideas. We must be willing to let it all go. We must become as defenselessly, innocently devoid of knowing *anything* as little children are. Then the magic happens. Then the miracles are revealed.

Seeing into the Issue: The Path Ahead

Here is my best encouragement to you: Go slowly. Conditioning is going to want to turn this into a contest. You have the tools to see for yourself, to prove to yourself that simply sitting still and watching what goes on—disidentifying and coming to center—creates a space, a distance that enables you not to take it all so personally. As you take each step to awakening from the bondage of ignorance and delusion, it will not be possible to cause you not to know what you know, but it could be possible to distract you and get you caught up in a side issue while egocentricity reconfigures its troops.

See if you can just stay with each step, noticing everything and believing nothing. Notice what the voices tell you, notice your emotional reactions, notice what the voices have to say about the emotions, notice what you have a tendency to get hooked by, and notice where the sensations are in your body. See if you can avoid the temptation to make any of what you see *mean* anything or need to *result* in anything. Just stay with the noticing.

Here's a summary you can use to continue this process for yourself.

1. Choose an issue you want to work with.

2. Sit down, stay still, and be aware of all that goes on.

3. Notice what belief systems are held in place with this issue.

4. Notice which subpersonalities are involved.

5. Listen to what the voices have to say about the issue and about who you are for having it.

6. Become aware of the projections made onto yourself and others because of this issue.

7. Explore the emotions that keep this issue real.

8. Find out where the issue is held in your body—where is the epicenter?

9. Practice disidentifying by moving your focus of attention away from the issue and returning it to the breath.

10. Remember to do this—and everything you do—in a context of compassionate acceptance of all that is.

Small steps. Having a life you want is a by-product of disidentification from egocentric conditioning. It's like happiness in that way. We pay attention, we find our willingness to accept, embrace, and let go; we work at dropping everything and returning to the breath, to the moment; and at some point, someone says something such as, "You seem happy"—and upon reflection, you can see why someone would reach that conclusion. For yourself, you are probably just aware of feeling grateful and saying thank you a lot.

When voices start saying things such as, "You aren't going to see anything new," or "Why don't you just give up on this?," you can just note those as well.

As many times a day as you can, just stop what you're doing and look inward. Who's here? What am I talking to myself about? What is my mood? What reality is being reinforced? What illusion am I caught in? Who is asking these questions? Who is looking? Breathing. Breathing. Breathing. Where is my attention? Can I stay with the breath? What arises to capture my attention?

All of the conditioning, the trauma, and the defenses have had not one iota of effect on your essential being—on your true nature and your authentic being, which simply *is*. All the misery and suffering that has happened has done nothing to who you are. Everything we seek is here when we stop doing anything other than being.

Let everything be exactly as is—nothing to do, nothing to get, nothing to be. Take a breath, and let it go. Can we let it be that simple?

Can we recognize the tension, the resistance, the arguments, the stress, the striving, the anxiety, the fear, the wants, and the deprivation for what it is—the desperate clinging of an illusion trying to maintain a life separate from life?

Can we be open to the possibility that there is nothing wrong? Can we find the willingness to consider that all of life is a treasure beyond imagining, a beautiful gift to enjoy?

We can.

❋ ABOUT THE AUTHOR ❋

Cheri Huber has been a student and teacher in the Soto Zen tradition for over 25 years. She is the founder of, and teacher-in-residence at, the Zen Monastery Practice Center in Murphys, California. She travels throughout the country and beyond conducting workshops and retreats. Her gentleness, clarity, and humor provide support for the challenging and joyous work of spiritual growth. She is the author of ten books, including: *The Key and the Name of the Key Is Willingness, There Is Nothing Wrong with You, The Depression Book, The Fear Book,* and *Be the Person You Want to Find.* Cheri is also one of the featured authors in *The Fabric of the Future: Women Visionaries Illuminate the Path to Tomorrow,* published by Conari Press.

The Zen Monastery Practice Center, where Cheri Huber teaches, offers a full schedule of workshops and retreats. Topics include meditation practice, compassionate self-acceptance, fear, joy, awareness through art, aspects of the self, depression, and many others. Contact the center in one of the following ways to receive a current schedule.

Write: P.O. Box 1979, Murphys, CA 95247
Call: (209) 728-0860
Fax: (209) 728-0861
E-mail: zencentr@volcano.net
Website: keepitsimple.org

To purchase meditation supplies, call Keep It Simple at: (800) 337-3040. For a one-year subscription to our quarterly newsletter, *In Our Practice*, send a check for $12, along with your name and address.

❋ Notes ❋

✺ Notes ✺

❋ Notes ❋

❈ Notes ❈

�֎ Notes ✤

❇ Notes ❇

Hay House Titles of Related Interest

Absolute Happiness
The Way to a Life of Complete Fulfillment,
by Michael Domeyko Rowland

The Alchemist's Handbook,
by John Randolph Price

The Experience of God
How 40 Well-Known Seekers Encounter the Sacred,
edited by Jonathan Robinson

Infinite Self
33 Steps to Reclaiming Your Inner Power, by Stuart Wilde

Pathways to the Soul
101 Ways to Open Your Heart, by Carlos Warter, M.D., Ph.D.

You Can Heal Your Life,
by Louise L. Hay

(All of the above titles are available at your local bookstore, or
may be ordered by calling Hay House at 800-654-5126.)

Please visit the Hay House Website at: **www.hayhouse.com**

❊ ❊ ❊

We hope you enjoyed this Hay House book. If you would
like to receive a free catalog featuring additional
Hay House books and products, or if you would like
information about the Hay Foundation, please contact:

Hay House, Inc.
P.O. Box 5100
Carlsbad, CA 92018-5100

(760) 431-7695 or (800) 654-5126
(760) 431-6948 (fax) or (800) 650-5115 (fax)
www.hayhouse.com

❊ ❊ ❊

Published and distributed in Australia by:
Hay House Australia Pty. Ltd. • 18/36 Ralph St. • Alexandria NSW 2015
Phone: 612-9669-4299 • *Fax:* 612-9669-4144 • www.hayhouse.com.au

Published and distributed in the United Kingdom by:
Hay House UK, Ltd. • Unit 62, Canalot Studios
222 Kensal Rd., London W10 5BN • *Phone:* 44-20-8962-1230
Fax: 44-20-8962-1239 • www.hayhouse.co.uk

Published and distributed in the Republic of South Africa by:
Hay House SA (Pty), Ltd., P.O. Box 990, Witkoppen 2068
Phone/Fax: 2711-7012233 • orders@psdprom.co.za

Distributed in Canada by:
Raincoast • 9050 Shaughnessy St., Vancouver, B.C. V6P 6E5
Phone: (604) 323-7100 • *Fax:* (604) 323-2600

❊ ❊ ❊

Sign up via the Hay House USA Website to receive the Hay House online
newsletter and stay informed about what's going on with your favorite authors.
You'll receive bimonthly announcements about: Discounts and Offers, Special
Events, Product Highlights, Free Excerpts, Giveaways, and more!
www.hayhouse.com